SHADOW
OF
AN AGONY

THE HIGHEST GOOD

PUBLISHING BOOKS THAT FEED
THE SOUL WITH THE WORD OF GOD.

CHRISTIAN LITERATURE CRUSADE
Fort Washington, Pennsylvania 19034

THE SHADOW OF AN AGONY

THE HIGHEST GOOD

OSWALD CHAMBERS

"Through the Shadow of an Agony comes Redemption"

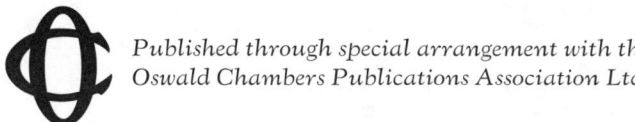

Published through special arrangement with the
Oswald Chambers Publications Association Ltd.

The Shadow of an Agony
Copyright ©1934 by Oswald Chambers Publications Association

The Highest Good
Copyright ©1937 by Oswald Chambers Publications Association

This edition copyright ©1992 by Oswald Chambers Publications Association Limited

Unless indicated otherwise, Scripture quotations are from The New King James Version. Copyright © 1979, 1980, 1982, Thomas Nelson, Inc., Publishers.

Discovery House Publishers is affiliated with Radio Bible Class, Grand Rapids, Michigan

Discovery House books are distributed to the trade by Thomas Nelson Publishers, Nashville, Tennessee 37214

All rights reserved.

ISBN: 0-929239-53-9

Printed in the United States of America

92 93 94 95 / CHG / 10 9 8 7 6 5 4 3 2

CONTENTS

The Agony of Redemption 13

The Conscience of God 22

The Conscience of Christ 31

The Christian Conscience 41

In Thought 51

The Dance of Circumstances 61

The Pressure of the Present 73

The Psychological Phase—I 83

The Psychological Phase—II 91

Humanity and Holiness 102

The Pilgrim's Song Book 111

    Psalm 120 113

    Psalm 122 118

    Psalm 123 124

    Psalm 124 129

    Psalm 125 134

    Psalm 126 139

Psalm 127 143

Psalm 128 148

The Highest Good 153

Summum Bonum 155

Righteousness 163

Missing It 170

Irresponsibility 179

The Base Impulse 187

The Base Impulse (continued) 196

Your Great Redemption 203

Foreword 205

Redemption 206

Redemption: The Christian's Greatest Trust 209

Relative Redemption Reactions 212

"The Lord God Omnipotent Reigns" 216

The Ruling Issues of Redemption 219

The Character of Redeemed Experience 221

The Magnitude of Redemption 225

Actually Born into Redemption 229

Dimensions of Effective Redemption 232

Publisher's Foreword

Although Oswald Chambers ministered before and during the First World War (1914-18), his frequent references to "the war" serve to reveal the relevance of his message rather than assigning it to the archaic past. The catastrophe that war is, certainly including wars of the recent past, reminds us of our fallenness and our desperate need of redemption. Personal calamity reinforces that awareness and confronts us individually with the need to be delivered from this pilgrimage of death. The theme of this book is to show the magnificence of that redemption, the wonder-filled agony of God by which He provided the Deliverer and through Him forgiveness and new birth.

In his own inimitable style, Chambers probes deeply into the great themes of scriptural revelation as he seeks the answer to the problem of pain and suffering, not as a systematic theologian but as a man "of the book" for whom the Bible was the only textbook. Because of his confidence in the authority of the Word, and his constant focus on Jesus Christ as our Redeemer, the publishers are honored to present this newly combined edition of two very significant books in the "Oswald Chambers Library," *The Shadow of an Agony* and *The Highest Good*.

The Publisher

Preface to First Edition

Two classes of readers will take up this little book of Bible studies on vital questions relating to Christian character and conduct and the mystery of suffering. The one class will find in it, as did even Peter in Paul's epistles, things hard to be understood, and sentences that lull the stolid mind to sleep; the other class will read, mark, learn, and inwardly digest its contents because they challenge mind and conscience, and will do their "utmost for the Highest." The author is a lover of men's souls: he sees into the heart of things, rises above the commonplace, and goes below the surface. "The war," he says, "has upset every man's nest; we are face to face with a terrific upheaval in life; there is no civilized security anywhere on the globe. We have seen that there is no such thing as a Christian nation, we have seen the unutterable futility of the organized Christian church, and many a man who has had no tension in his life has been suddenly obliged to face things he never intended to look at." These very things Oswald Chambers shows us in the light of the Cross. He points out that because Jesus Christ is so like unto His brethren we can face this turmoil and stress, and stand with Him in the shadow of a great agony, undiscouraged and unafraid. There is really only one mystery in the universe; it is the mystery of redemption. The way we approach this holy ground is nearly always through suffering. Those that carry the cross after Jesus best understand why and how He first carried it, and how the nails pierced not His hands only but His heart.

To the careless and superficial this book will only appeal when they gird up the loins of their minds and are sober. Once they put on the girdle which Paul calls "sincerity" and Peter "humility," its message will grip, convince, and appeal, as it did when first delivered to the men of all ranks in the Y.M.C.A. camps and huts of Egypt.

> Great truths are greatly won,
> Not found by chance,
> Nor wafted on the breath of summer dream,
> But buffeting with adverse winds and tides.
>   Samuel M. Zwemer

Cairo, 1918.

Foreword to the Fourth Edition

It is some years ago since a copy of *The Shadow of an Agony* came into my hands. How it did so I do not now remember. I know, however, that I started to read it with no great expectation of profit. But I soon found I had made a real discovery. The little book was a truly great book; its author a truly great man. Since then I have read and pondered every published utterance by the Rev. Oswald Chambers, and am grateful for the intellectual stimulus and spiritual quickening that have come to me from his writings. His "passing hence" was a great loss to the Christian church.

For the times in which we live I know of no work more fitting for re-publication than *The Shadow of an Agony*. It deals with root or rock principles. It comes, not from the surface, but "out of the depths." It is the work of a great brain and a great heart. It does not shirk the problems of life, but looks them straight in the face. Over against the tragedy of sin and suffering it brings us to the tragedy of the Cross of Christ.

In the hope that the book will prove to be as great a discovery and as great an inspiration to others as it has been to me, I write this Foreword.

> Walter H. Armstrong
> First Moderator of the Free Church
> Federal Council of England and Wales
> Ex-President of Methodist Conference

Norwich, September, 1942

The Agony of Redemption

Oh, to have watched Thee through the vineyards wander,
    Pluck the ripe ears and into the evening roam,
Followed and known that in the twilight yonder
    Legions of angels shone about Thy home.

Ah, with what bitter triumph had I seen them,
    Drops of Redemption bleeding from Thy brow,
Thieves and a culprit crucified between them,
    All men forsaking Him, and that was Thou.

(1) *Approaching the Holy Ground* (Exodus 3:5; Joshua 5:15; Psalm 119:67, 71, 75; Jeremiah 31:18-19; Hebrews 12:5-11). "The truth of Christianity cannot be proved to the man in the street till he comes off the street owning its power."

(2) *Apprehending the Holy Grace* (Romans 5:7-9; Hebrews 5:7-9). "Christianity is concerned with God's holiness before all else, which issues to men as love, acts upon sin as grace, and exercises grace through judgment."

(3) *Atonement by the Holy God* (Matthew 1:21; Acts 20:28; 2 Corinthians 5:14-21).

By centrality is meant finality for human history and destiny.... It is meant, first, that in the atonement we have primarily an act of God and an act of God's holiness; second, that it alone makes any repentance or expiation of ours satisfactory to God; third, that as regards man it is a revolutionary act and not a mere stage in evolution (Dr. Forsyth).

If we estimate things from the standpoint of a man's life, redemption will seem "much ado about nothing." But when we come to a big Judgment Day like a European war, when individual lives apparently amount to nothing, and human lives are being swept away by the thousand, the "bottom board" is knocked out of our ignorance, and we begin to see that the basis of things is not rational, but wild and tragic. It is through these glimpses that we understand why the New Testament was written, and why there needed to be a redemption made by Jesus Christ, and how it is that the basis of life is redemptive. If Jesus Christ were only a martyr, His Cross would be of no significance; but if the Cross of Jesus Christ is the expression of the secret heart of God, the lever by which God lifts back the human race to what it was designed to be, then there is a new attitude to things.

(1) *Approaching the Holy Ground.*

Then He said, "Do not draw near this place. Take your sandals off your feet, for the place where you stand is holy ground" (Exodus 3:5).

There is a moral preparation necessary to face the truth of God. These words of God to Moses mean literally, "Stand further off and you will see better." Sometimes our moods are mean and ignoble; at other times they are lofty and good.

To a large extent a man's moods are not in his own power.

> We cannot kindle when we will
>   The fire that in the heart resides;
> The spirit bloweth and is still,
>   In mystery our soul abides.
> But tasks in hours of insight will'd
> Can be through hours of gloom fulfilled.

"Strip off your commonplace moods," God says; "if you are going to see into this thing, you must put on the right mood for discerning it." The agony of a man's affliction is often necessary to put him into the right mood to face the fundamental things of life. The psalmist says, "Before I was afflicted I went astray, but now I keep Your word." The Bible is full of the fact that there has to be an approach to the holy ground. If I am not willing to be lifted up, it is no use talking about the higher heights. In putting John the Baptist to death, Herod committed moral suicide. He ordered the voice of God to be silent in his life, and when Jesus Christ stood before him, "he questioned with Him in many words," for "he hoped to see some miracle done by Him"; but we read that Jesus "answered him nothing." It is quite possible for any man among us to get to a place where there is no such thing as truth or purity, and no man gets there without himself being to blame. Every man ought to be intellectually skeptical, but that is different from moral doubt which springs from a moral twist. No man can do wrong in his heart and see right afterward. If I am going to approach the holy ground, I must get into the right frame of mind—the excellency of a broken heart.

The war has upset everyone's nest, and we are face to face with a terrific upheaval in life; there is no civilized security anywhere on the globe. We have seen that there is no such thing as a Christian nation, and we have seen the unutterable futility of the organized Christian church: and many a man who has had no tension in his life has been suddenly dumped "into the soup" and been obliged to face things that he never intended to look at. Consequently, there are any number of amateur skeptics and men who are seeing the difference between "believing their beliefs" and "believing God," men, who, through the turmoil and the stress, are seeing that rationalism is not the basis of things. According to the Bible, the basis of things is tragedy, and the way out is the way made by God in redemption. The New Testament does not say that the human race is evolving, but that the human race is a magnificent ruin of what it was designed to be. God Himself has taken the responsibility of sin, and the proof that He did so is the Cross; God holds me responsible if I refuse to let Him deliver me from sin. No man can redeem the world; God has done it; redemption is complete. That is a revelation, not something we get at by thinking; and unless we grant that redemption is the basis of human life, we will come up against problems for which we can find no way out. The thing that will need to be restated after the war, theologically, is redemption; at present "redemption" is not in the vocabulary of the average earnest person.

Through the turmoil and agony that nations and men are in, men who think are beginning to see that rationalism is not the basis of things. The basis of things is not reasonable; reason is our guide among things as they are, but it never can account for things as they are. No man ever chose his own father and mother, or his own heredity; such things go clean through the "bottom board" of rationalism; they are illogical; there is a deep, real problem at the basis of them. The basis of things, according to the Bible, is tragic, and the way out is the way made by God in redemption, not by intellect or by reason. The revelation of New Testament Christianity deals with the basis of human life. Every one of us is shaken into the turmoil of things, caught by the last eddy, and we have to get some kind of foothold. In the meantime, don't be distressed at what men say, or at the tags they wear. "Talk to my meaning, not to my words." Don't be a debating logician and make a man mean what you mean; try to get at his mind behind the thing; and when you hear a man talk in agony, remember he is hurt. Be patient and reverent with what you don't understand.

(2) Apprehending the Holy Grace (Romans 5:7-9; Hebrews 5:7-9).

"Grace"—the overflowing favor of God. The way of approach to the holy ground of God is nearly always through suffering; we are not always in the natural mood for it, but when we have been plowed into by suffering or sorrow, we are able to approach the moral frontiers where God works. To apprehend the holy grace of God, I must remember that according to the New Testament, Jesus Christ is God manifest in the flesh. This fundamental revelation of the Christian faith seems to be overlooked among Christians. There is only one God for the Christian, and He is Jesus Christ. The Bible only mentions two men—Adam and Jesus Christ, and it is the last Adam who rehabilitates the human race.

During the war the stab has come to every one of us, and we are in an attitude to understand what the New Testament is talking about. Before the war it did not matter to the majority of us whether Jesus Christ lived or died, because our thinking was only within the circumference of our own lives. Now, through the war, we are seeing the need for redemption. The grace of God which comes through Jesus Christ is revealed in that God laid down His life for His enemies. The statement that a man who gives his life for his king and country thereby redeems his soul, is a misapprehension of New Testament revelation. Redemption is not a man's bit. "Greater love has no one than this, than to lay down one's life for his friend," has nothing to do with Christianity; an atheist will do this, or a blackguard, or a Christian; there is nothing divine about it, it is the great stuff that human nature is made of. The love of God is manifested in that He laid down His life for His enemies, something no man can do. Paul says the fundamental revelation of the New Testament is that God redeemed the whole human race when they were spitting in His face, as it were.

If you have had no tension in your life, never been screwed up by problems, your morality well within your own grasp, and someone tells you that God so loved you that He gave His Son to die for you, nothing but good manners will keep you from being amused. The majority of people who have never been touched by affliction see Jesus Christ's death as a thing beside the mark. When a man gets to his wits' end and things go hard with him, his thick hide is pierced and he is stabbed wide awake, then for the first time he begins to see something else. "At last I see; I thought that He was stricken, smitten of God and afflicted; but now I see He was wounded for my transgressions."

The great fundamental revelation regarding the human race is that God has redeemed us; and redemption enters into our lives when we are upset enough to see we need it. There is too much common sense used, "pills to cure an earthquake" given; and "the gospel of temperament" preached. It is an insult today to tell some men and women to cheer up. One of the most shallow petty things that can be said is that "every cloud has a silver lining." There are some clouds that are black all through. At the wall of the world stands God with His arms outstretched; and when a man or woman is driven there, the consolations of Jesus Christ are given. Through the agonies in human life we do not make redemption, but we see why it was necessary for God to make it. It is not necessary for every man to go through these agonies, but it takes a time of agony to get the shallow skepticism knocked out of us. It is a good thing to be reverent with what we do not understand. A moral agony gives a man "a second wind," and he runs better after it, and is a good deal more likely to win.

(3) Atonement by the Holy God (Matthew 1:21; Acts 20:28; 2 Corinthians 5:14-21).

The church is the new Spirit-baptized humanity based on the redemption of Jesus Christ. Intellectual rationalism is based on a volcano, and at any second it may be blown to pieces; but there is nothing below redemption; it is as eternal as God's throne. Redemption is a moral thing, Jesus Christ does not merely save from hell; "He will save His people from their sins," that is, make totally new moral men. Jesus Christ did not come to give us pretty ideas of God, or sympathy with ourselves; He came from a holy God to enable men, by the sheer power of His redemption, to become holy.

In the Christian faith the basis of human life is redemption, and on that basis God can perform His miracles in any man.

So long as we live in the "tenth story" we remain indifferent to the fact of forgiveness; but when we "strike bottom" morally, we begin to realize the New Testament meaning of forgiveness. Immediately a man turns to God, redemption is such that his forgiveness is complete. Forgiveness means not merely that I am saved from sin and made right for heaven (no man would accept forgiveness on such a level); forgiveness means that I am forgiven into a recreated relationship, into identification with God in Christ.

The background of God's forgiveness is holiness. If God were not holy there would be nothing in His forgiveness. There is no such thing as God overlooking sin; therefore if God does forgive there must be a reason that justifies His doing so. If I am forgiven without being altered by the forgiveness, forgiveness is a damage to me and a sign of the unmitigated weakness of God. When a man is convicted of sin he knows God dare not forgive him; if he did it would mean that man has a bigger sense of justice than God. God, in forgiving a man, gives him the heredity of His Son, i. e., He turns him into the standard of the Forgiver. Forgiveness is a revelation—hope for the hopeless; that is the message of the gospel.

A man may say, "I don't deny that God will forgive me, but what about the folks I have put wrong? Can God give me a 'clearing-house for my conscience?' " (Hebrews 9:14). It is because these things are neglected in the presentation of redemption that men are kept away from Jesus Christ. Men are kept away by honesty more than by dishonesty.

Jesus Christ's revelation is the forgiveness of God, and the tremendous miracle of redemption is that God turns me, the unholy one, into the standard of Himself, the Forgiver, by the miracle of putting into me a new disposition. The question up to me is—"Do I want Him to do it?" God's forgiveness is a bigger miracle than we are apt to think. He will not only restore to us the years the cankerworm has eaten; not only deliver us from hell; not only make a clearing house for conscience; but He will give a totally new heredity; and many a man who has shut himself down in despair need not despair any more. God can forgive a man anything but despair that He can forgive him.

These are the fundamentals of human life. We have not been taught to think as Christians, and when an agony reaches us we are knocked to pieces, and only hang on by the skin of our teeth. We may have faith enough to keep us going, but we do not know where to put our feet or to tell anyone else where to put theirs. We have been taught to think as pagans, and in a crisis we act as pagans. It is a great thing to have a spiritual experience, but another thing to think on the basis of it. The great fundamental point of view in the Bible is neither rationalism nor common sense. Either it is a revelation, or it is unmitigated blather. The basis of life is not mathematical or rational; if it were we could calculate our ends, and make absolutely sure of certain things on clear, rational, logical lines. We have to take into account the fact that there is an incalculable element in every child and in every man. There is always "one fact more," and we get at it by agony.

The Conscience of God
Hebrews 6:13

Thou with strong prayer and very much entreating
    Willest be asked, and Thou shalt answer then,
Show the hid heart beneath creation beating,
    Smile with kind eyes and be a man with men.

Were it not thus, O King of my salvation,
    Many would curse to Thee and I for one;
Fling thee Thy bliss and snatch at Thy damnation,
    Scorn and abhor the shining of the sun.

(1) The Creator Aspect (Genesis 1:27; Psalm 82:6; John 10:34-35; Luke 3:38). God (Intellectual): Because God is Creator and we are His creatures, nothing else matters.

(2) The Cosmic Aspect (Genesis 1:1; Job 38:4-7; Isaiah 42:5; Acts 17:24). God (Emotional): The emotions produced by natural actualities are no end-all.

(3) The Culture Aspect (Psalm 50:21; Isaiah 44:14-17; Colossians 2:18-23). God (Educational): The refined findings of intellect and emotions; all else to be disdained.

(4) The Christian Aspect (John 3:16; 2 Corinthians 5:18-21). God (Evangelical): Complete forgiveness and final redemption.

It is not necessary for a man to understand things before he can be a Christian. The understanding of the mystery of life is a secondary thing; the main thing is to be alive. Science is an understanding of life and the universe. If a man said he had no use for science, we should reckon him to be a fool. It is the same with regard to the Christian religion. The important thing is to be a born-again man. Theology is the science of religion, an intellectual attempt to systematize the consciousness of God. Intellect systematizes things to a man's mind, but we do not reach reality through intellect. Theology comes second, not first, and ought always to be open to dispute. Because science and theology have been put in the wrong place, it is foolish to say we will have nothing to do with them. Redemption is not a thing we are consciously experiencing, it is a revelation given by the Christian religion of the basis of human life, and it takes some thinking about. We don't think on Christian lines at all.

"For when God made a promise to Abraham, because He could swear by no one greater, he swore by Himself" (Hebrews 6:13). Conscience is not the voice of God; conscience is that faculty in me which appeals to the highest I know; it may or may not be religious. God has a conscience toward human beings and toward Himself, that is, He has a standard to keep, and the problem He is up against is not to wipe the muddle off the slate, but to resolve it back again, and redemption is His way of doing it. To try and explain redemption in the span of a person's life is nonsense. People may not feel the need of redemption, but that does not mean it is not there. The Christian revelation is the revelation of why redemption was necessary. God's standard is to make of human beings the counterpart of Himself; people have to be brought into perfect communion with God. At present there is an enormous hiatus between God and man, and God's conscience in redemption puts man back again into the purpose for which He designed him, instead of wiping him out and saying it is all a muddle. The highest standard God has is Himself, and it is up to God to make a man as good as He is Himself; and it is up to me to let Him do it. If God is not just, the only honorable thing for a man to be is a blatant atheist.

Agony means severe suffering in which something dies—either the base thing, or the good. No one is the same after an agony; we are either better or worse, and the agony of our experience is nearly always the first thing that opens our minds to understand the need of redemption worked out by Jesus Christ.

(1) *The Creator Aspect (Genesis 1:27).*

God created man, the federal head of the human race, in his own image; we are procreated through generations of the human race; Adam was created in the image of God. The male and female together, as they were created, were in the image of God, in perfect union with God. "Adam and Eve" are both needed before the image of God can be perfectly presented.

The Creator aspect appeals to a man's intellect as long as he has no memory of the Fall and the ruin that followed when the connecting link with Deity was snapped. If you develop yourself in your brain and say, "That is 'myself,' " you have to shut yourself off from life as it actually is, and on that line you can manipulate anything, and construct the most extraordinary things. An intellectual God does not amount to "a row of old beans." The creator aspect of God ignores everything else; it forgets that the Bible gives revelations of God on other lines. The Bible says that God created the federal head of the race in His own image; that means that God accepts the responsibility for the human race being put on the wrong track, and the Cross is the proof that He does so. I seal myself with damnation when I see the Light, Jesus Christ, and prefer my own standpoint. The Creator aspect of God does not amount to much. If the only aspect of God is that of Creator, to talk about a moral or spiritual life is nonsense; but the Creator aspect is not the complete Christian aspect; it is only one ingredient in it.

(2) *The Cosmic Aspect (Genesis 1:1).*

Cosmic means the order of the material universe produced by actualities. The Creator aspect is a fact; the Cosmic aspect is also a fact; but there are other aspects. If I build my thinking on the Creator or the Cosmic aspect only, I have to miss some factors out. If I take an intellectual view of life only, I shall come to the conclusion that Thomas Carlyle came to; he judged people by brains and came to the conclusion that half the human race were fools. If the intellectual valuation of human beings be the right one, when he is insane he should be killed. The brain is the thing that makes a person express himself; but a person is more than his consciousness. The intellect says, "I will have nothing to do with what I cannot explain intellectually." A man's intellect is his instrument, his guide among things as they are; but it never gave him things as they are. There is more to be taken into consideration before you get the right view of God and man.

(3) *The Culture Aspect (Isaiah 44:14-17).*

This aspect says that God is the result of an educated mind, and that we get at God by abnormal means—by education, mysticism, and aestheticism; if so, then atheism is saner.

Isaiah says that a man takes a tree and cuts it in two, uses part to cook his food, and the other part he carves into an idol to worship. "None of us do that!" we say; but we do. There are other things which are wooden besides trees, namely, our heads! We use one half of our heads to earn our living, and the other half to worship God.

These three aspects of God amount to nothing more than a man produces by his own nature, and have not nearly so much power over him as he has over himself. If I want to get at reality my conscience must witness as well as my emotions. I may talk like an archangel and live like a pig; I may write magnificent stuff, and have fine conceptions, and people may be thrilled, but that does not prove that I have touched reality. A man's intellect may give him noble ideas, and power to express them through his soul in language, but it gives him no power to carry them out in action. When a man has touched reality, he is changed into its image. Intellect has never changed a man as yet; it may have made him look different, but it will not have altered him. If intellect is the way to get to God, what about the men who have no intellect? There would be whole streaks of man's life and experience to blot out. Or if I can get at God by a fine sense of beauty only what about the men who have no sense of beauty? Some men have a magnificent heredity, while others are practically damned into existence. Rationalism is not the basis; my reason and my intellect are instruments, but there is something deeper about every human life than can be fathomed by intellect. The God constructed out of the Culture aspect does not amount to anything. Thinking is an abstraction whereby man locates the things he sees. The laws of nature have no existence outside the intellect of the scientist, and to talk about Jesus Christ transcending the laws of nature is nonsense. A law is a method of explaining things in an ordered intellect. You can dispute a man's reasoning, but you cannot dispute facts; they must be accepted. If you deal only with these three aspects, you remain out of touch with reality, because each aspect does only for the view it presents. If the aspect of God is to be colored by refined intellect, some of us will never get there. If everybody were refined it would be all right, but everybody is not, and the Culture aspect treats the rest of the human race with disdain.

(4) *The Christian Aspect (2 Corinthians 5:18-21).*

In the Christian aspect we have these three other aspects worked in with another view: the conscience of God and the New Testament insistence on the Cross of Jesus Christ. The attitude of the Bible to the human race is not a common sense one. The Christian aspect deals with man as a specimen of a human race which is a magnificent ruin of what it was designed to be. Supposing the view of the Bible to be right, to whom is it "up to" to right the wrong? The Creator. Has He done it? He has, and He has done it absolutely single-handed. The tremendous revelation of Christianity is not the Fatherhood of God, but the Babyhood of God—God became the weakest thing in His own creation, and in flesh and blood He levered it back to where it was intended to be. No one helped Him; it was done absolutely by God manifest in human flesh. God has undertaken not only to repair the damage, but in Jesus Christ the human race is put in a better condition than when it was originally designed. It is necessary to understand these things if you are to be able to battle for your faith. "The Deity of the Christian religion is evidenced by the variety of fools who tackle it." Today we are erecting a man of straw, and then taking it for granted that the Author of salvation was a fool. Jesus Christ's view is that the Christian religion has been tried and abandoned, but never been tried and failed. It is not a question of whether we agree with the Bible revelation or not, but of whether we take it for what it reveals before we tackle it.

God's conscience means He has to forgive completely and finally redeem the human race. The point about Christian forgiveness is not that God puts snow over a dung heap, but that He turns a man into the standard of the Forgiver. The great thing up to God is that in forgiving me He has to give me the heredity of His Son. God Himself has answered the problem of sin and there is no man on earth but can be presented "perfect in Jesus Christ."

Redemption does not amount to anything to a man until he meets an agony; until that time he may have been indifferent; but knock the bottom board out of his wits, bring him to the limit of his moral life, produce the supreme suffering worthy of the name of agony, and he will begin to realize that there is more in redemption than he had ever dreamed, and it is at that phase that he is prepared to hear Jesus Christ say, "Come unto Me." Our Lord said, "I did not come to call the man who is all right; I came to call the man who is at his wits' end, the man who has reached the moral frontier."

> Oh, could I tell, ye surely would believe it!
>   Oh could I only say what I have seen!
> How should I tell or how can ye receive it,
>   How, till He bringeth you where I have been?

A man will know sooner or later; it will depend upon the pride of his intellect or the crass obstinacy of his nature how soon he gets there; but when he does he will have reached the frontier where God works. Never keep your moral nature skeptical. Never doubt that justice and truth and love and honor are at the back of everything, and that God must be all these or nothing. The Christian aspect is that God will make a man as holy as He is Himself, and this He has undertaken to do. If a man is terrified by the vastness of creation, he has never been touched by the moral problem. When he has, he knows that God created the universe for him. God created man to be master of the life in the earth and sea and sky, and the reason he is not is because he took the law into his own hands, and became master of himself, but of nothing else. Man is a remnant of a former design. In the conscience of God that design is restored. The "Creator" and the "Cosmic" and the "Culture" aspects are all etceteras to the main thing, we enter into touch with God on the frail, human-experience, moral line. The Christian aspect of God represents the One Who has been in the very thick of it; and whenever a man through nature or through conviction of sin touches the moral frontiers, then the work of Jesus Christ begins.

"If anyone is in Christ, he is a new creation (2 Corinthians 5:17). I see the universe as a mirror of my ruling disposition. I see in sunsets and sunrises and in the whole cosmic force an exaggerated expression of the ruling disposition in myself; I do not see God, I see myself. When I am born from above, I see the reflection of God. The disposition ruling within me determines the way I interpret outside things. A man convicted of sin and a man in love may live in the same external world, but in totally different creations. Both may be in the desert, but the disposition of the one makes him interpret the desert as a desolating piece of God's territory; while to the other the desert literally blossoms as the rose. The disposition of the one is mad; there is no light in the sun, no sweetness in anything, his ruling disposition is one of misery; while to the other:

> Heaven above is brighter blue,
> >   Earth around is sweeter green:
> Something lives in every hue
> >   Christless eyes have never seen;
> Birds with gladder songs o'erflow,
> >   Flowers with deeper beauties shine
> Since I know, as now I know,
> >   I am His and he is mine.

When you are identified with Jesus Christ you become a new creation in the same surroundings. You see life differently because of the moral transfiguration of the regeneration of the Son of God. The conscience of God means that it is up to Him to make this possible, and any man can go through the transfiguration the second he realizes his need. There are moments when you see the way you should go; don't dally with yourself then. The moments come and go, but always with a further space between. If you play the fool with yourself when they come, they get fainter; but if you heed them, they are intimations that you are stepping over into another frontier, and beginning to experience a relationship to God based on the Cross of our Lord Jesus Christ.

The Conscience of Christ

> Christ! I am Christ's! and let the name suffice you,
>   Ay, for me too He greatly hath sufficed;
> Lo! with no winning words I would entice you,
>   Paul has no honor and no friend but Christ.
>
> Yes thro' life, death, thro' sorrow and thro' sinning
>   He shall suffice me, for He hath sufficed;
> Christ is the end, for Christ was the beginning,
>   Christ the beginning, for the end is Christ.

(1) The Character of Christ (Matthew 11:19; Acts 2:22-24)
"The New Testament never thinks that the place which Jesus has in its faith is anything else than the place which belongs to Him and truly was His" (Dr. Denney).

(2) The Consciousness of Christ (Matthew 5:21-22, 27-28, 38-39, 43-44; 11:27; John 8:46; 14:6-9)
"Jesus revealed Himself as what He was in life and works; He had to be discovered as what He was by men who associated with Him in obedience, trust, and love" (Dr. Denney).

(3) The Cross of Christ (Matthew 16:24; 20:22; 26:12-13, 26-28; Romans 5:11)
"The Christ that we trust all to is One in whom God died for His own witness and His own work in us. God was in Christ reconciling. The prime doer in Christ's Cross was

God; He was God doing the very best for man, and not man doing his very best for God" (Dr. Forsyth).

It is in times of intense suffering that we begin to see the reason for redemption, and realize that redemption is worth what it cost the original Designer. According to the New Testament, redemption cost God everything, and that is the reason why salvation is so easy for us. The same thing happens in an agony as happens when you suddenly open your door and window during a hurricane; the wind disarranges everything. It plays havoc, and knocks things into confusion, but also brings a totally new circulation of air; and very often the man who has been knocked around by an agony begins to form a new mind, and is better able to appreciate the New Testament view of the Cross of Jesus Christ.

The basis of God's action is that it is up to Him to turn out men like himself, and the conscience of Christ also means just that. To say that reason is the basis of human life is absurd, but to say that the basis of human life is tragedy and that the main purpose of it as far as Jesus Christ is concerned, is holiness, is much nearer the point of view given in the Bible.

(1) *The Character of Christ (Matthew 11:19; Acts 2:22-24).*

These verses portray the character of Jesus Christ as recorded in the New Testament. The New Testament is not written to prove that Jesus Christ is God Incarnate; the New Testament does not prove anything; it simply confirms the faith of those who believe beforehand. Christian evidences don't amount to anything; you can't convince a man against his will.

"The New Testament never thinks that the place which Jesus had in its faith is anything else than the place which belongs to Him and truly was His" (Dr. Denney).

The New Testament does not say of Jesus Christ, "This man was God Incarnate, and if you don't believe it you will be damned." The New Testament was written for the confirmation of those who believed He was God Incarnate. The man who does not believe is apt at any minute to discover by the swinging open of the door of agony, that the thing he ignored may be the way into a life he has never seen. It is quite likely that a trick of disease or war or bereavement may suddenly open the possibility of there being other things in a man's story than those he saw when he was a common-sense, robust man.

"The Son of Man came eating and drinking." One of the most staggering things in the New Testament is just this commonplace aspect. The curious difference between Jesus Christ's idea of holiness and that of other religions lies here. The one says holiness is not compatible with ordinary food and married life, but Jesus Christ represents a character lived straight down in the ordinary amalgam of human life, and His claim is that the character He manifested is possible for any man, if he will come in by the door provided for him.

There are religions in which holiness involves unusual conditions and special diet. Some forms of mysticism seem to be incompatible with married life. But the type of holiness which Jesus teaches can be achieved with an ordinary diet and a wife and five children. (*The Jesus of History,* T. R. Glover)

We must estimate the character of Jesus Christ by the New Testament, and not by our standards. Look at the ordinary commonplace things of His life—from twelve to thirty years of age. He lived with brothers and sisters who did not believe in Him (John 7:5). If you had lived in His day and someone had pointed Him out and said to you, "That carpenter is God manifest in the flesh," you would have thought him mad. The New Testament is either unmitigated blather or it conveys a revelation. The majority of us make the character of God out of our own heads; therefore He does not amount to anything at all. That God is called an omnipresent, omniscient, omnipotent Being who rules the universe does not matter one iota to me. But the new Testament reveals the essential nature of God to be not omnipotence, omnipresence, and omniscience, but holiness. God became the weakest thing in His own creation— a baby; He entered human history on that line. He was so ordinary that the folks of His day paid no attention to Him, and the religious people said He was making a farce of religion.

> Jesus Christ is, beyond all reasonable question, the greatest Man who ever lived. The greatness of a man is to be estimated by two things; first, by the extent of his influence upon mankind, and secondly— for no one is altogether great who is not also good— by the purity and dignity of his character. Tried by both these tests, Jesus is supreme among men. He is at once the most influential and the best of Mankind (*The Fact of Christ,* P. Carnegie Simpson).

To refuse to try a line Jesus Christ points out because I do not like it shuts my mouth as an honest doubter. I must try it and see if it works. As long as I am unwilling to act by any way of getting at the truth, I can say nothing.

The basis of Christ's character appeals to us all. One of the dangers of denominational teaching is that we are told that before we can be Christians we must believe that Jesus Christ is the Son of God, and that the Bible is the Word of God from Genesis to Revelation. Creeds are the effect of our belief, not the cause of it. I do not have to believe all that before I can be a Christian; but after I have become a Christian I begin to try and expound to myself who Jesus Christ is, and to do that I must first of all take into consideration the New Testament explanation. "Blessed are you, Simon Bar-Jona, for flesh and blood has not revealed this to you, but my Father who is in heaven."

The character of Jesus Christ was lived on an ordinary plane, and exhibits one side only. To ten men who talk about the character of Jesus there is only one who will talk about His Cross. "I like the story of Jesus Christ's life, I like the things He said. The Sermon on the Mount is beautiful, and I like to read of the things Jesus did"; but immediately you begin to talk about the Cross, about forgiveness of sins, about being born from above, I am out of it." The New Testament reveals that Jesus Christ is God manifest in the flesh, not a Being with two personalities; He is Son of God (the exact expression of Almighty God) and Son of Man (the presentation of God's normal man). As Son of God He reveals what God is like (John 14:9); as Son of Man He mirrors what the human race will be like on the basis of redemption—a perfect oneness between God and man (Ephesians 4:13). But when we come to the Cross of Jesus Christ, that is outside our domain. If Jesus Christ was only a martyr, the New Testament teaching is stupid.

(2) The Consciousness of Christ (Matthew 5:21-22, 27-28, 38-39, 43-44; 11:27; John 8:46; 14:6-9).

These verses express what Jesus Christ thought about Himself. He deliberately said, "Before I came, Moses said; now I have come I say; up till now it has been so-and-so; but I interpret in a new way." If He was not God manifest in the flesh, to speak like that would have been an intoxication of conceit. Let Plato or Socrates, for instance, say, "I am the Way, the Truth, and the Life," and we see what it involves. Jesus Christ is either mad or what He claims to be: the only revelation of God Almighty there is. Our Lord did not say, "No one comes to God except through Me," but, "No one comes to the Father except through Me." Fatherhood and Creatorship are two different things. Fatherhood refers to the moral likeness of a man's disposition.

In the conscience of God and in the conscience of Christ we see God accepting the responsibility for sin; He never asks man to accept it. No man is damned because he is a sinner, Jesus said, "This is the condemnation [that is, the critical moment], that the light has come into the world, and men loved the darkness rather than light, because their deeds were evil" (John 3:19). If I see better than I act on, I am sealing my soul with damnation. The consciousness of Jesus Christ in the New Testament is that He and the Father are one; He did not say that the human race and God were one. The doctrine of the Trinity is not a revelation, it is an attempt to put into scientific language the fact of God. There is only one God to the Christian, and His name is Jesus Christ; any other idea of God is a matter of temperament or of refinement. The Christian is an avowed agnostic; all he knows about God has been accepted through the revelation of Jesus Christ, and to him there is only one name for the

God he worships, namely, Jesus Christ. Jesus Christ manifests, on the scale we see and know, the life that makes Him say—"Almighty God is nothing that contradicts what I am; if you have seen Me you have seen the Father." Have we seen Him? We may look at a person for a long time without "seeing" him. How long did it take the men who knew Jesus Christ to perceive Who He was? (Luke 24:16, 31).

Both these themes, the character and the consciousness of Christ, are in the nature of speculation—interesting, but they do not amount to anything when a man is in agony. When we were plunged into the agony of the war, modern Christianity was dealing with speculations, or else proclaiming a pseudo-evangelism which made salvation a moral "lavatory." Jesus Christ did not come primarily to teach; He came to make it possible for us to receive His heredity, to have put into us a new disposition whereby we can live totally new lives. Any man who uses his reason in the things he sees, and who has taken a cross section of himself, and had the conceit knocked out of him, knows he is not a strayed angel nor a noble hero; he is neither angel nor devil; he is a mixture of dust and deity. The Sermon on the Mount is impossible to man, and yet it is what our Lord taught. Jesus Christ did not come to teach man to be what he cannot be, but to reveal that He can put into him a totally new heredity; and all he requires a person to say is—"I need it"—no shibboleth, but a recognition of his need. Jesus Christ cannot begin to do anything for a man until he knows his need; but immediately he is at his wits' end through sin or limitation or agony and cannot go any further, Jesus Christ says to him, Blessed are you; if you ask God for the Holy Spirit, He will give Him to you. God does not give us the Holy Spirit until we come to the place of seeing that we cannot do without Him (Luke 11:13).

(3) The Cross of Christ (Matthew 16:24; 20:22; 26:12-13, 26-28; Romans 5:11).

There are two views of Jesus Christ's death. One is that He was a martyr—that is not the New Testament view; the other is that the Cross of Jesus Christ was the Cross of God, not of a man at all—not a man doing his level best for God, but "God doing the very best for man." The Cross of Jesus Christ is the point where God and sinful man merge with a crash, and the way to life is opened; but the crash is on the heart of God. The Cross is the presentation of God having done His "bit," that which man could never do. The New Testament reveals that the basis of human life is not rationalism, but redemption. Just as rationalism does not depend on individual people but on a conception of the fundament of human life, so the New Testament represents that the basis of human life is redemption, and Christian faith and Christian thinking are to be based on that. There is much teaching abroad today that is veneered over as Christianity. Men preach, and undermine the very ground they stand on while they preach. The foundation of the Christian faith is that the basis of human life is redemptive, and on that basis God performs His miracles. Jesus Christ told His disciples that He came here on purpose to die. The death of Jesus Christ is God's verdict on self-realization and every form of sin there is. If self-realization is to be the goal and end of the human race, then damned be God; if Jesus Christ is to be God, then damned be self-realization—the two cannot exist together. "If you would be My disciple, give up your right to yourself."

Why should we play at being Christians? We are told that to be an experimental Christian means we understand the plan of salvation; the devil understands that, but he is not a saint. A saint is one who, on the basis of the redemption of Jesus Christ, has had the center of his life radically altered, and has deliberately given up his right to himself. This is the point where the moral issue comes, the frontier whereby we get in contact with God. Intellect will not bring us there, but moral obedience only, and an agony opens the door to it. To those who have had no agony Jesus says, "I have nothing for you; stand on your own feet, square your own shoulders. I have come for the man who knows he has a bigger handful than he can cope with, who knows there are forces he cannot touch; I will do everything for him if he will let Me. Only let a man grant he needs it, and I will do it for him."

This is the basis of what Jesus Christ did in redemption, and we enter into the life of Christ by His death, not by His birth. When Jesus Christ taught His disciples these things, and when He talked about His Cross, they misunderstood Him, just as natural minded Christians do today; consequently we are up against the problem already mentioned. The teaching of Jesus Christ is very fine and delightful, but it is all up in the clouds; how are we to come up to it with our heredity, with what we are with our past, with our present and with the outlook we have? How are we going to begin to do it, if all He came to do was to teach? All attempts at imitation will end in despair, in fanaticism, and in all kinds of religious nonsense. But when once we see that the New Testament emphasizes Jesus Christ's death, not His life, that it is by virtue of His death we enter into His life, then we find that His teaching is for the life He puts in.

"We also rejoice in God through our Lord Jesus Christ, through whom we have now received the reconciliation" (Romans 5:11). As long as we are intellectualists and forget that we are people, our intellect tells us that God and man ought to be one, that there should be no gap between. Exactly so! But they are not one, and there is a gap, and a tragedy.

Our intellect tells us that the universe ought to be the "garment of God." It ought to be, but it is not. We may hold any number of deistic and monistic theories, and theories about being one with God, but every man knows he is not God. Jesus Christ says we can only receive the at-one-ment with God on His basis: "Unless one is born again, he cannot see the kingdom of God" (John 3:3). We can enter into His Kingdom whenever the time comes for us to see it. We cannot see a thing until we do see it, but we must not be blind and say we don't see it when we do, and if we are enthusiastic saints we must not be too much disturbed about the fellow who does not see. At any second he may turn the corner of an agony and say, "I thought those other fellows were mad, but now I am prepared to see as they do."

We have been taken up with creeds and doctrines, and when a man is hit we do not know what to give him; we have no Jesus Christ, we have only theology. For one man who can introduce another to Jesus Christ by the way he lives and by the atmosphere of his life, there are a thousand who can only talk jargon about Him. Whenever you come across a man or woman who in your time of distress introduces you to Jesus Christ, you know you have struck the best friend you ever had, one who has opened up the way of life to you.

The basis of human life according to Jesus Christ is His Cross, and it is by His Cross that His conscience is manifested. He has undertaken to take the vilest piece of stuff that humanity and the devil have put together, and to transform this into a son of God. If I receive forgiveness and continue to be bad, I prove that God is immoral in forgiving me, and make a travesty of redemption. When I accept Jesus Christ's way He transfigures me from within. "Jesus did it all," refers to redemption; the thing is done; and if I step into it I will find the moral magic of the redemption at work in me.

The Christian Conscience

> Great were his fate who on the earth should linger,
>   Sleep for an age and stir himself again,
> Watching Thy terrible and fiery finger
>   Shrivel the falsehood from the souls of men.
>
> Oh that Thy steps among the stars would quicken!
>   Oh that Thine ears would hear when we are dumb!
> Many the hearts from which the hope shall sicken,
>   Many shall faint before Thy kingdom come.

N. B. The intuition in my nature whereby I know that I am known.
The intuition in my nature which I regard as the highest.
The "innocence of sight" as an illustration of conscience.

(1) *Conscience before the Racial Degeneration*
(Genesis 2:7-17).
    (a) Implicit Certainty of Self (v. 7).
    (b) Implicit Certainty of the World (v. 8-15).
    (c) Implicit Certainty of God (v. 16-17).
    The race was required to take part in its own development by a series of moral choices till transfiguration.

(2) *Conscience after the Racial Degeneration*
(Romans 1:18-27).

(a) Standard of the Ordinary Person (Romans 2:14-16).
(b) Standard of the Ordinary Pagan (Matthew 25:31-46).
(c) Standard of the Ordinary Piety (John 16:2; Acts 26:9).

Virtuous in order to secure one's self if God should be awkward.

(3) *Conscience in the Racial Regeneration* (John 3:16-21).

(a) Character of the Saint (John 17:22; Romans 9:1).
(b) Conduct of the Saint (2 Corinthians 1:12).
(c) Communion of the Saints (1 John 1:7).

Personal relation with God is to be maintained in actual experience by the spontaneous originality of the indwelling Spirit of God, interpreting the words of Christ as we obey.

Intuition means perception at sight; it is implicit, something I cannot express, and conscience is of the implicit order of things. Conscience is the innate law in human nature whereby man knows he is known. Conscience is that faculty in me which fixes on what I regard as the highest; consequently conscience records differently in different people. I may be a Christian and a conscientious man, or I may be an atheist and a conscientious man. So it never can be true to call conscience the voice of God; if it were, it would be the most contradictory voice man ever heard.

Conscience is best thought of as the eye of the soul recording what it looks at; it will always record exactly what it is turned toward. We soon lose what Ruskin called "the innocence of sight." An artist does not use his logical faculties in recording what he sees; he records from the innocence of sight. A beginner sketches not what he sees, but what he knows he sees, while the artist gives the presentation of what he sees. Conscience is the eye of the soul, and how my conscience records will depend on the light that is thrown on God. Saul of Tarsus was conscientious in putting to death the followers of Jesus Christ (Acts 26:9); when he became a Christian, his conscience was not altered, but it recorded differently (Acts 24:16). When a man gets rightly adjusted to God his conscience staggers him, and his reason condemns him from all standpoints. The phrase "conscience can be educated" is a truth that is half an error. Strictly speaking, conscience cannot be educated; what is altered and educated is a man's reasoning on what his conscience records. A man reasons not only on what his senses bring him, but on what his conscience brings him; and immediately he is faced by the white light of Jesus Christ, his conscience recording exactly, his reason is startled and amazed.

(1) Conscience before the Racial Degeneration (Genesis 2:7-17).

In this aspect we have to consider the three facts of a man's personal life: consciousness of self, consciousness of the world, and consciousness of God; they are all brought out in the way God constituted the human race. Adam had no affinity with the animals, and this instantly distinguished him from the creation around him—"But for Adam there was not found a helper comparable to him." There is no evidence that an animal is conscious of itself, but man is ostensibly conscious of himself.

We are conscious of ourselves and conscious of outside things only by means of a nervous system. When a man is altered inwardly by the grace of God, his nervous system is altered, and he instantly begins to see things differently. The external world around him begins to take on a new guise because he has a new disposition. "If anyone is in Christ," his nervous system will prove that he is "a new creation," and the material world will appear to him as a new creation because he is now seeing it as the mirror of God's thought.

The God-consciousness in Adam was quite different from our natural consciousness; it was just like the God-consciousness shown by our Lord. In us the consciousness of God is obliterated, because that consciousness became most conspicuously blurred by the Fall; consequently, men miscall all kinds of things "God." A man is apt to call any system of things he considers highest "God."

There are three facts of our personal life that are restored by Jesus Christ to their pristine vigor. We get into real definite communion with God through Jesus Christ; we get to right relationship with our fellow-men and with the world outside; and we get into a right relationship with ourselves. We become Christ-centered instead of self-centered.

If Adam had not sinned and thereby introduced the heredity of sin into the human race, there is every reason to suppose that the human race would have been transfigured into the real presence of God; but Adam disobeyed, and sin entered in. Sin is a relationship between two of God's creations. God did not create sin; but He took the responsibility for it; and that He did so is proved in the Cross of Jesus Christ. The essential nature of sin is my right to myself. Jesus Christ, the last Adam, the second Federal Head of the race, entered into this order of things as Adam did, straight from the hand of God; and He took part in His own development until it reached its climax, and He was transfigured. Earth lost its hold on Him, and He was back in the glory which He had with the Father before the world was. But He did not go to heaven from the Mount of Transfiguration because He had redemption to fulfill. He emptied Himself of His glory a second time, and came down into the world again to identify Himself with the sin of man (2 Corinthians 5:21).

Adam was intended by God to take part in his own development by a series of moral choices, to sacrifice his natural life to God by moral obedience and thus transform it into a spiritual thing. Instead, he took dominion over himself, and instantly lost control over the earth and air and sea, and lost also this peculiar consciousness of himself and the world and God. Poetic and intellectual types of mind recognize these factors in Adam's creation, but they ignore the fact that we have degenerated. A poet or an artist has vision and insight, but he does not see the actual. It is delightful to talk about man being in perfect accord with God and with the world about him; but we are not in that accord, and the guidance God gave to Adam is of no use to us.

We can change the world without when we change the recording instrument within. Commit sin, and I defy you to see anything beautiful without; fall in love, and you will see beauty in everything. We only know the world by a nervous system, and we infer that everyone else knows it in the same way as we do. The man who accepts things on the evidence of his senses is as wise as I am when I accept the revelation of the Bible. To accept the evidence of your senses is wise, but to say it is infallible is nonsense. It is never wise to be cocksure.

(2) Conscience after the Racial Degeneration (Romans 1:18-27).

"Everyone is to blame but me; I am a strayed babe in the wood!" This attitude indicates the twist in man's nature that has come in through the Fall. A moral squint always leads to a wrong intellectual view.

(a) Standard of the Ordinary Person (Romans 2:14-16). Everyone has, implicit within himself, a standard of conduct which he accepts for life. There is an intuitive certainty in everyone that there are some things that he ought not to do, and the talk about innocence is nonsense. The Bible says that a person is born with this knowledge, and that he will be judged according to his obedience to, or rejection of, the ordinance of God which is written in his spirit. The natural idea of virtue is to make a man quits with the Day of Judgment.

(b) Standard of the Ordinary Pagan (Matthew 25:31-46). The standard for the nations is conscience, that is, conscience attaching itself to the system of things which people regard as highest, no matter how degraded they may be. Conscience is the standard for men and women to be judged by until they have been brought into contact with the Lord Jesus Christ. The standard for Christians is not Matthew 25; the standard for Christians is our Lord Jesus Christ. It is not sufficient for a Christian to walk in the light of his conscience; he must walk in a sterner light, in the light of the Lord.

(c) Standard of the Ordinary Piety (John 16:2; Acts 26:9). Paul says, "Indeed, I myself thought [that is, according to his conscience] I must do many things contrary to the name of Jesus of Nazareth." This is the length an ordinary pious conscience may take a man. Saul was the acme of conscientiousness. It is extraordinary to what an extent people may corrupt themselves if they have no real light on what they regard as the highest. There needs to be a standard for the guidance of conscience. It does not matter whether a person is religious or not, conscience attaches itself to the highest he or she knows, and reasoning according to that standard is the guide for life. Conscience will always record God whenever it has been faced by God.

(3) Conscience in the Racial Regeneration (John 3:16-21).

I am not judged by the light I have, but by the light I have refused to accept. There is no man but can have the knowledge, perfectly clearly obtainable, of the standard of Jesus Christ. Whether I am a Christian or not, or whether I am conscientious or not, is not the question; it is whether I have refused the light of the finest moral character who ever lived, Jesus Christ. This is the condemnation, that the Light, Jesus Christ, has come into the world, and I prefer darkness, that is, my own point of view. The characteristic of one who begins to walk in the light is that he drags himself into the light all the time. He does not make excuses for things done in the dark, he brings everything to the light, and says, "This is to be condemned; this does not belong to Jesus Christ," and so keeps in the light. The popular view of a saint is an anemic young man with one foot in the grave, or an old woman, or an innocent, sweet young lady—anyone who has not enough original sin to be bad. The New Testament view of a saint is a more rugged type. You and I are a mixture of dust and deity, and God takes that sordid human stuff and turns it into a saint by regeneration. A saint does not mean a man who has not enough sin to be bad, but a man who has received from Jesus Christ a new heredity that turns him into another man.

(a) Character of the Saint (John 17:22; Romans 9:1). The Christian development keeps its balance with the law of God, which is holiness. A man's character is what he habitually is. What "glory" did Jesus Christ have? A glory that everyone could see and admit that He was a marvelous Being? No, He was so ordinary that they said He was a glutton and a wine-bibber; so ordinary that fishermen walked with Him, and the common people asked Him to dinner.

There was no glory externally; He was not manifestly God walking in the flesh. Jesus Christ effaced the God-head in Himself so effectually that men without the Spirit of God despised Him. The glory our Lord had here on earth was the glory of a holy disposition; that is, He worked out His life in accordance with the highest He knew—His Father; and He said, "I can give people that faculty in regeneration; I can put My Holy Spirit in them, and He will keep them in contact with God as I have revealed Him." Conscience and character in the saint, then, means the disposition of Jesus Christ persistently manifested.

(b) Conduct of the Saint (2 Corinthians 1:12). Paul always riddled himself like that; he did not talk to people who did not know him. He said, "The evidence of my life proves that what Jesus Christ said He could do, He has done." (See Galatians 2:20.)

"Our rejoicing is this, the testimony of our conscience, that in simplicity and godly sincerity . . . we have had our conversation in the world." The point there is a very important one—that the knowledge of evil that came through the Fall gives a man a broad mind, but paralyzes his action. The restoration of a man by our Lord gives him simplicity. Paul says, "I fear, lest somehow . . . your minds may be corrupted from the simplicity that is in Christ." There are men and women of the world who know evil, whose minds are poisoned by all kinds of things; they are marvelously generous in regard to their notions of other people, but they can do nothing, their broad-sightedness paralyzes their action. There are some things a person is a criminal for knowing; he has no right to know them. The knowledge of evil, instead of instigating to action, paralyzes; whereas the essence of the gospel of Jesus Christ working in conscience and conduct is that it shows itself at once in action. God can turn cunning, crafty people into simple, guileless people. The marvel of His grace is such that He can take out the strands of evil and twistedness from a person's mind and imagination, and make him single-minded and simple toward God so that his life becomes radiantly beautiful by the miracle of His grace.

(c) *Communion of the Saints (1 John 1:7).* "But if we walk in the light, as He is in the light . . ." that is, don't have anything folded up, don't juggle things, don't pretend you have not done anything shady. John says, if you have committed sin, confess it; walk in the light, and you will have fellowship with everyone else who is there. Natural affinity does not count here at all. Watch how God has altered your affinities since you were filled with the Spirit; you have fellowship with people you have no natural affinity for at all; you have fellowship with everybody who is in the light. Light is the description of clear, beautiful, moral character from God's standpoint, and if we walk in the light, "The blood of Jesus Christ cleanses us from all sin;" God Almighty can find nothing to censure.

We usually think of conscience as an individual thing; the individual aspect has to be recognized, but it is not the only aspect. The individual exercise of conscience is never the Christian standard. The Christian standard is the personal relationship of the conscience in direct accord with God on the basis of the revelation given by Jesus Christ. I do not live the Christian life by adherence to principles; I live the Christian life as a child lives its life. You never can calculate what a child will do, neither can you calculate what the Spirit of God will do in you. When you are born from above, the Spirit of God in you works in spontaneous moral originality. Our Lord said, "the Holy Spirit . . . will teach you all things, and bring to your remembrance all things that I have said to you." I do not rake around and discover some word; the Holy Spirit brings back with the greatest of ease the word I need in a particular circumstance. Am I going to obey that word? If we keep our individual consciences open toward God as He is revealed in Jesus Christ, God will bring hundreds of other souls into oneness with Himself through us.

This is the way the new racial regenerated conscience is to come about. Racial conscience is not the conscience of the individual person, but the conscience of a whole community of people who are in touch with God.

In Thought

> Be near me when my light is low,
>   When the blood creeps, and the nerves prick
> And tingle; and the heart is sick,
>   And all the wheels of Being slow.
> Be near me when the sensuous frame
>   Is rack't with pangs that conquer trust;
> And Time, a maniac scattering dust,
>   And Life, a Fury slinging flame.

(1) *In the Whirlwind of Things that Are*
  (a) Quarrels of Nations (Luke 21:10-11).
  (b) Quarrels of Churches (1 Corinthians 3:1-5).
  (c) Questions of the Way On (Matthew 24:23-26).

(2) *Internationals of Socialism, Sacerdotalism, and Spirituality*

(3) *Federations Most Hopeful*

"Amid the quarrels of nations is it not wonderful that many minds, untutored either in history or in ethic, should seek to find it in some form like socialism which is indifferent to Nationality, and which overrides the concrete divisions of mankind by abstract ideas and artificial associations, while others, only too historic, find it in a church unity over their heads" (Dr. Forsyth).

If we are faced with a problem, we cannot be indifferent. The greatest help we can give to another is not a positive line of things, but this warning: Don't seal up your mind too quickly.

(1) *In the Whirlwind of Things that Are.*

> You will hear of wars and rumors of wars. See that you are not troubled (Matthew 24:6).

That is either the statement of a madman or of a Being who has power to put something into a man and keep him free from panic, even in the midst of the awful terror of war. The basis of panic is always cowardice. Our Lord teaches us to look things full in the face. He says—"When you hear of wars, don't be scared." It is the most natural thing in the world to be scared, and the clearest evidence that God's grace is at work in our hearts is when we do not get into panics. Our Lord insists on the inevitableness of peril. He says, "You must lay your account with war, with hatred, and with death." Men may have lived undisturbed over a volcano for a long while, when suddenly an eruption occurs. Jesus Christ did not say, "You will understand why war has come," but, "Don't be scared when it does come, do not be in a panic." It is astonishing how we ignore Jesus Christ's words. He said that nations would end in war and bloodshed and havoc. We ignore His warnings; and when war comes we lose our wits and exhibit panic.

(a) *Quarrels of Nations (Luke 21:10-11).* This question is on the lips of people today: "Is war of the devil or of God?" It is of neither. It is of man, though both God and the devil are behind it. War is a conflict of wills, either of individuals or of nations. National quarrels are everywhere today and it is these quarrels which make men say—"Well, blot out nations altogether; the only thing to do is to ignore the fact that there are nations; let us look forward to a time when there will be none." This attitude is a revolt which is a mere safety valve. The vision of a time when there will be no nations is right, but ignoring the fact that there are nations just now is not the way to establish the vision.

After the war the elemental will take its place again, and we shall recover what we had lost in over-civilization. Civilized life will be all the better for the clearing out of some things, and there are some things we shall regret losing. We shall be driven back to the elemental; we shall be a good deal less refined, more rugged; more like our own country five hundred years ago. In the final issue some things belonging to civilization will be found to be fine, and some disastrous. The preaching of the "gospel of temperament" and all such shallow optimism has been hit on the head by the war; there are some clouds with no "silver lining," and the injunction to "cheer up" is an insult.

(b) *Quarrels of Churches* (1 Corinthians 3:1-5). It is easy to see the defects in churches. I may criticize my own church, but let me remember that her defects are those of immaturity. A person may be full of defects, but we must remember that there is a difference between the vices of a man and the failings of a boy. When we see the powerlessness as ineffectiveness of the churches, we are apt to revolt to sacerdotalism, which is priestcraft being used as an exotic over human nature. Frequently, religious peace has been brought about in this way, but it has not been a desirable peace. When men are compelled to submit to superstition, they are apt to say, "Let us have no churches at all, or else let us have a democratic church."

(c) Questions of the Way On (Matthew 24:23-26). "If anyone says to you, 'Look, here is the Christ!' or 'There!' do not believe it." Today we have all kinds of Christs in our midst, the Christ of Labor and of Socialism; the Mind-cure Christ and the Christ of Christian Science and of Theosophy; but they are all abstract Christs. The one great sign of Christ is not with them—there are no marks of the Atonement about these Christs. Jesus Christ is the only One with the marks of atonement on Him, the wounded hands and feet, a symbol of the Redeemer who is to come again. There will be signs and wonders wrought by these other Christs, and great problems may be solved, but the greatest problem of all, the problem of sin, will not be touched.

The majority of us are blind on certain lines, we see only in the light of our prejudices. A searchlight lights up only what it does and no more, but the daylight reveals a hundred and one facts that the searchlight had not taken into account. An idea acts like a searchlight and becomes tyrannous. Take a man with an idea of evolution; as you listen to him the way seems perfectly clear, life is not difficult at all; but let the daylight of actual experience come across his path, and there are a thousand and one facts which the idea cannot account for, because they do not come into the simple line laid down by the evolutionist. When I am up against problems, I am apt to shut myself up in my own mind and refuse to pay any attention to what anyone says. There are many things that are neither black nor white, but gray. There is nothing simple under heaven saving a man's relationship to God on the ground of the redemption of Jesus Christ. When Jesus Christ came on the scene, His disciples became impatient and said, "Why don't You tell us plainly who You are?" Jesus Christ could not, because He could only be discerned through moral obedience. A man who talks like a shell makes the path of a shell, that is, he makes the way straight, but destroys a good deal in doing it. There is another way of reaching the solution of a problem—the long, patient way of solving things. Jesus Christ deliberately took the "long, long trail." The temptation of Satan was that He should take the "short cut." The temptations of Satan center around this point: "You are the Son of God, then do God's work in Your own way"; and at the heart of all our Lord's answers was this: "I came to do My Father's work in His way, not in My own way, although I am the Son of God."

A fanatic sees God's point of view but not man's. He says God ought not to allow the devil, or war, or sin. We are in the whirlwind of things that are, what is the use of wasting time and saying things ought not to be? They are! In the midst of the problems, what is the way out? The line of solution is not to apply the plaster of a philosophical statement, or the principles of teetotalism, or of vegetarianism, but something more fundamental than these: a personal relationship to God and Man as one—Jesus Christ. "Don't make principles your aim, but get rightly related to Me," Jesus Christ says.

The revelation of Christianity is that God, in order to be of use in human affairs, had to become a typical Man. That is the great revelation of Christianity, that God Himself became human; became incarnate in the weakest side of His own creation. If one can put it reverently, unless God Almighty can become concrete and actual, He is nothing to me but a mental abstraction, because an ideal has no power unless it can be realized. The doctrine of the Incarnation is that God did become actual, and that He manifested Himself on the plane of human flesh. Jesus Christ is not only the name of the personal Savior who made the way for every man to get back into that personal relationship, but He is the name for God and Man in one. "Son of Man" means the whole human race centered in one personality. Jesus Christ declares that He is the exclusive way to the Father (John 14:6; Matthew 11:27).

A religious fanatic says, "I will work from the Divine standpoint and ignore the human." You cannot do it; God Himself could not do it. He had to take upon Himself "the likeness of sinful flesh." There must be the right alloy. You cannot use pure gold as coin, it is too soft to be serviceable, and the pure gold of the Divine is no good in human affairs; there must be the alloy mixed with it, and the alloy is not sin. Sin, according to the Bible, is something that has no right in human nature at all, it is abnormal and wrong. Human nature is earthly, it is sordid, but it is not bad. The thing in human nature that is bad is the result of a wrong relationship set up between the man God created and the being God created who became the devil, and the wrong relationship whereby a man becomes absolute "boss" over himself is called sin. Sin is a wrong element, an element that has to be dealt with by God in redemption through man's conscience.

The fanatical person is certain that human beings can live a pure Divine life on earth. But we are not so constituted, we are constituted to live the human life presenced with Divinity on earth, on the ground of redemption. We are to have the right alloy—God and humanity one, as in our Lord Jesus Christ. That is the miracle of the redemption when it works actually in human flesh. The way out is to remember that the alloy must be discovered in you and me—the pure Divine working on the basis of my pure human. I may have the most beautiful sentiments in prayer and visions in preaching, but unless I have learned how God can mix the human and the Divine and make them a flesh and blood epistle of His grace, I have missed the point of Jesus Christ's revelation.

(2) *Internationals of Socialism, Sacerdotalism, and Spirituality.*

Socialism at present is immensely vague, it is the name for something which is all right in vision, but the point is how is the vision to get legs and walk? How are we going to establish the peace of the world so that nations will not go to war any more, or grab at each other? How are we going to arrive at an equality that will work? How is it to be done? These are the last days of a dispensation from God's standpoint. (The Bible dispensations are not things we note, they are marked off by the Spirit of God. Today militarism has gone into hell before the eyes of the whole world.) "And it shall come to pass in the last days, says God, that I will pour out of My Spirit on all flesh [irrespective of goodness or badness]; . . . And on My menservants and on My maidservants I will pour out My Spirit in those days." What is the difference between "your sons and your daughters" and "My menservants" and "My maidservants?" "Your sons and your daughters" refer to the men and women who have no concern about the redemptive point of view: "We have the vision and we are going to do the thing in our own way." Peter says God is long-suffering, and He is giving us ample opportunity to try what ever line we like in both individual and national life. God is leaving us to prove to the hilt that it cannot be done in any other than Jesus Christ's way, or the human race will not be satisfied.

The atheist, or socialist, or Christian—all who look to the future and express a view of what ought to be, see the same vision. They see the brotherhood of humankind, a time of peace on earth when there will be no more war, but a state of goodwill and perfect liberty, at present inconceivable. There is nothing wrong with the vision, and there is no difference in the vision because its source is the Spirit of

God; the difference is in the way it is to be reached. The vision is of the nature of a castle in the air. That is where a castle should be; who ever heard of a castle underground! The problem is how to put the foundation under your castle in the air so that it can stand upon the earth. The New Testament says that the only foundation is not rationalism but the absolute efficacy of the redemption of Jesus Christ. We are not prepared to see that yet; there may be individuals who are, but no nation under heaven is. It is a long process for an individual to centralize his mind on Jesus Christ's standpoint, and it must take nations a long while too. The socialist in his domain is like the fanatic in the Christian domain; he is apt to see the vision and forget the problem— forget that in the meantime we are not there! After the war we shall have to be down among the demon-possessed, and then will be the time to prove whether we can give legs to our vision. Locusts, in their flight, will tumble down in the streams and drown by the million, but others keep coming on until they bank the stream right up, and the live ones crawl over the piled-up dead. Hundreds of men in the past twenty centuries have had the vision, and given their lives for it. No one thinks anything about them now, but it is over the lives of these men that the rest of us are beginning to crawl and find a footing.

Sacerdotalism has proven a quick way out of a good many difficulties. It says: "Put the incubus of a church rule on the nations and say, 'You shall do this'; unite temporal and Divine power under an infallible head." It is one way of holding peace for a time, but it is a peace that does not grow from the inside of solving the problems of men; it comes from the outside, like an extinguisher, on to the problems and says, "I am the infallible church in the line of the Apostolic Succession; you shall not doubt, I will solve all your problems." In every period when the nations have been held in peace, it has been by an external authority, such as a church, acting like an exotic, spreading its roots over the mass of humanity and holding it together. The Roman Catholic Church is a proof of this. There is only one thing as futile as the Roman Catholic Church and that is Protestantism. In Roman Catholicism the great dominating authority is Churchianity, the church is vested with all authority. In Protestantism it is what the Book says that is the supreme authority, and a person gets rest when he decides for either. "I am going to give up all the turmoil and let my church do my thinking for me." If you put your faith in a church, it will solve your problems for you. Or you may stake your faith in Bibliolatry with the same result. "You search the Scriptures, for in them you think you have eternal life; and these are they which testify of Me. But you are not willing to come to Me that you may have life" (John 5:39-40). Jesus Christ says neither the church nor the Bible is the authority, but "I am the way, the truth, and the life"; the church and the Bible are secondary. The context of the Bible is Jesus Christ, and a personal relationship with Him interprets the Bible in a person's life. There are ways of bringing peace to a person's mind that are not true to the fundament of things, and one of the most significant things during the war is the change of mental front on the part of men as they face these things.

(3) *Federations Most Hopeful.*

Another man says, "Federation is the most hopeful solution there is; not necessarily denominational union, but federations in spirit; let us look forward to the time when nations and denominations will be federated out of independent existence." This is, again, only a mental safety-valve.

Another man may say, "I believe in quiet mysticism, cutting myself off from everything around and getting at things by a spiritual life of my own." The monks in the Middle Ages refused to take the responsibilities of life by shutting themselves away from the world, and people today seek to do the same by cutting themselves off from this and that relationship. Paul says, "Beware of those who ignore the basis of human life." If I refuse to accept nations or churches or human beings as facts, I shall find I have nothing to help solve the problems that arise. We have to make the first footing clear. Is it possible, on the basis of redemption, to regenerate commerce? for Jesus Christ not to ignore the fact of men and women, but to regenerate them? for nations not to be ignored, but regenerated? Jesus Christ's claim is that it is possible. Jesus Christ was not deluded, nor was He a deceiver. He is the Way, the Truth, and the Life; and the only way out is by a personal relationship to Him. We are never exonerated from thinking on the basis on which Jesus Christ has put things by redemption.

The Dance of Circumstances

Nay but Thou knewest us, Lord Christ, Thou knowest,
    Well Thou rememberest our feeble frame,
Thou canst conceive our highest and our lowest,
    Pulses of nobleness and aches of shame.

Therefore have pity! not that we accuse Thee,
    Curse Thee and die and charge Thee with our woe;
Not thro' Thy fault, O Holy One, we lost Thee,
    Nay, but our own,—yet hast Thou made us so!

(1) *Personal Decisions for Christians*
    (a) Sin (destroyed) (1 John 3:8).
    (b) Sensuality (denied) (Romans 8:13; Colossians 3:3-6).
    (c) Sentimentality (ignored) (Luke 6:46).
    (d) Sensibilities (controlled) (John 17:15; Romans 14:20-23).

(2) *Providential Discretions for Christians*
    (a) The Mischief of Absorption (Galatians 4:16-20).
    (b) The Mistiness of Abstractions (1 Corinthians 5:9-13).
    (c) The Meaning of Affiliation (1 Peter 2:13-17).

"Without a country ye are bastards of humanity; without a country ye have neither name, token, voice, nor rights; no admission as brothers into the fellowship of peoples" (Mazzini).

"Through the shadow of an agony comes redemption." In a supreme agony something dies, no man is the same after it. The majority of us live our lives untouched by an agony; but in war, the chances are that all are hit somewhere, and it is through a personal agony that a man is likely to begin to understand what the New Testament reveals. As long as we have our morality well within our own grasp, to talk about Jesus Christ and His redemption is "much ado about nothing," but when a man's thick hide is pierced, or he comes to his wits' end and enters the confines of an agony, he is apt to find that there is a great deal from which he has been shut away, and in his condition of suffering he discovers there is more in the Cross of Christ than intellectually he had thought possible.

Beware of believing that the human soul is simple; look at yourself, or read Psalm 139, and you will soon find the human soul is much too complex to touch. When an intellectualist says that his life is simple, you may be sure he is sufficiently removed from facts to have no attention paid to him. Things look simple as he writes about them, but let him get "into the soup," and he will find they are complicated. The only simple thing in human life is our relationship to God in Christ.

Circumstances are the things that twist a man's thinking into contortions.

(1) *Personal Decisions for Christians.*

One of the first things we discover in dealing with the big universal problem is that it is mirrored in each individual life. When we are young we are all metaphysicians, we don't deal with physical things, but with things behind the physical. The young mind seems more competent than the middle-aged mind, because the latter has come the length of dealing with facts. The metaphysician and the philosopher deal only with abstractions which are supposed to explain facts. It is always the young mind that attempts to deal with the big universal problems; but when the young mind has had a dose of the plague of its own heart, the problem of the universe is obliterated by another, that of its own personal life, and if a solution can be found for that, it has a solution for the problems which lie further afield. The problem of the universe is not mine but the Almighty's; the problem I am up against is the muddle inside. Can I see a way out there? Is the God I have only an abstraction? If so, don't let me treat Him as anything else. Or is He One with whom I can get into a personal relationship, One who will enable me to solve my problems?

A Christian is a disciple of Jesus Christ's by the possession of a new heredity (John 3:3), one who has been brought into personal relationship with Jesus Christ by the indwelling Spirit of God, not one with certain forms of creed or doctrine; these are the effects of his relationship not the ground of it.

The man who brings with him any conception of God (especially if he is a Scotsman) will bring a conception based on Calvinism, a God described by the "Omni's." That God does not amount to anything to me. If I start out and say that the essential nature of God can be defined as omnipotence, omniscience, and omnipresence, I shall end by proving that Jesus Christ is a liar, for He was not omnipotent and omniscient and omnipresent when He was on earth; yet He claimed to be the complete revelation of God—"He who has seen Me has seen the Father." Either my theology is wrong or Jesus Christ is. If Jesus Christ is right, I must be prepared to revise my theology and say that those terms simply express certain manifestations which I called God. But if the essential nature of God is holiness, then I can see how it is possible for Jesus Christ to be God manifest in the flesh. The doctrine of the Incarnation means that God became the weakest thing in His own creation, a baby. The doctrine of the Trinity is not a Christian revelation, it is an attempt on the part of the mind of man to expound the Christian revelation, which is that there is only one God to the Christian, and His name is Jesus Christ.

A Christian is an avowed agnostic because he has accepted what he knows about God on the ground of revelation; he has not found it out for himself.

(a) *Sin (1 John 3:8)*. According to Jesus Christ, the first decision is that sin has to be destroyed. The first great moral effect of Jesus Christ's coming into the world is that He saves His people from their sins; not simply that He saves them from hell and puts them right for heaven; that is the finding of a Protestant evangel, not the New Testament view, and is only one phase of salvation. The great purpose of Jesus Christ's coming is that He might put man on a line where sin in him can be destroyed (1 John 2:1). The test of a Christian, according to the New Testament, is not that a man believes aright, but that he lives as he believes, that is, he is able to manifest that he has a power which, apart from his personal relationship to Jesus, he would not have. We all know about the power that spoils our sin, but does not take away our appetite for it. The first great decision to be made is that the only thing to do with sin is to destroy it, and the incoming of Jesus Christ enables a man to destroy the wrong relationship in himself.

(b) *Sensuality (Romans 8:13; Colossians 3:3-6)*. Sensuality is not sin, it is the way my body works in connection with external circumstances whereby I begin to satisfy myself. Sensuality will work in a man who is delivered from sin by Jesus Christ as well as in a man who is not. I do not care what your experience may be as a Christian, you may be trapped by sensuality at any time. Paul says, "Mortify the deeds of the body" (KJV). *Mortify* means to destroy by neglect. One of the first big moral lessons a man has to learn is that he cannot destroy sin by neglect; sin has to be handled by the redemption of Jesus Christ, it cannot be handled by me. Heredity is a bigger problem than I can cope with; but if I will receive the gift of the Holy Spirit on the basis of Christ's redemption, he enables me to work out that redemption in my experience. With regard to sensuality, that is my business; I have to mortify it, and if I don't, it will never be mortified. If I take any part of my natural life and use it to satisfy myself, that is sensuality. A Christian has to learn that his body is not his own. "Do you not know that your body is the temple of the Holy Spirit . . . and you are not your own?" Watch that you learn to mortify.

If I have an intellectual puzzle, I must see that I run it correspondingly with moral obedience. If I am perplexed about God's real universe, have I begun to make personal decisions about sin and sensuality? Every religious sentiment that is not worked out in obedience, carries with it a secret immorality; it is the way human nature is constituted. Whenever I utilize myself for my own ends, I am giving way to sensuality, and it is done not only physically, but mentally also, and one of the most humiliating things for a Christian is to realize how he does it. The impertinence of mental sensuality lies in the refusal to deny the right of an undisciplined intelligence that is contrary to Jesus Christ.

If I am going to find out a thing scientifically, I must find it out by curiosity; but if I want to find out anything on the moral line, I can only do it by obedience. God put man in a garden with the tree of knowledge of good and evil, and said, "You shall not eat of it." God did not say they were not to know good and evil, but that they were not to know good and evil by eating of the tree. They were intended to know evil in the way Jesus Christ knew it—by contrast with good. They did eat of the tree, consequently the human race knows good by contrast with evil. Adam knew evil positively and good negatively, and none of us knows the order God intended. No man who has eaten of the fruit of the tree knows evil by contrast with good. The curiosity of the human heart finds out the bad things first. The fruit of the tree of the knowledge of good and evil gives the bias of insatiable curiosity on the bad line, and it is only by the readjustment through Jesus Christ that the bias on the other line enters in—a tremendous thirst after God. Jesus Christ knew evil negatively by positively knowing good; He never ate of the tree, and when a man is reborn of the Spirit of God, that is the order.

(c) *Sentimentality (Luke 6:46).* Sentimentality is produced by watching things we are not in. We are all capable of being sentimental, that is, of living in a state of mind which produces emotions we do not intend to carry out. A hundred and one things will produce sentimentality—a cup of tea, a concert; a letter or a novel will do it. "I like to have my emotions stirred, but don't ask me to carry them out on their own level." If I allow an emotion and refuse to act it out on its right level, it will react on a lower level. The higher the emotion, the deeper the reaction; consequently, the higher the religious emotion, unless worked out on its own level, the more debased and appalling the reaction. That is why Paul connects sanctification with immorality, and why religious men fall much more bestially. Our guide as to what emotions we are going to allow is this—What will be the logical outcome of this emotion? If it has to do with sin and Satan, then grip it on the threshold of your mind and allow it no more way. You have no business to harbor an emotion the outcome of which you can see to be bad; if it is an emotion to be generous, then be generous, or the emotion will react and make you a selfish brute.

Sentimentality has to be ignored. Jesus Christ said, "You call Me Master and Lord, but you don't do what I say." That is the gist of the failure of Christianity; it has been tried and abandoned because it has been found difficult; but it has never failed when it has been tried and gone on with honorably. There is no problem or difficulty that stretches before a man for which adherence to Jesus Christ will not give him the line of solution.

(d) Sensibilities (John 17:15; Romans 14:20-23). "Sensibilities" means the things at the basis of life, the way we are naturally related to life. The three main sensibilities in a man's life are sex, money, and food. What has he to do with them? They are not sinful, they are plain facts which can be either devilish or sublime. Whenever Jesus Christ brought His teaching to a focus it was on two points, namely, marriage and money. In ordaining sex, God took the bigger risk and made either the most gigantic blunder or the most sublime thing. Sex has to be controlled, so have money and food. By what? By the highest. When God created the Federal Head of the race He required him to take part in his own development by a series of moral choices, whereby he was to sacrifice his natural sensibilities to the will of God and transform them.

Our Lord says He does not pray that His disciples shall be taken out of the world, but that they shall be kept from the evil one, kept from being overwhelmed. Paul, in Romans 14, beats out into gold foil what Jesus Christ gives in nugget form. He warns all through—Beware of those who teach abstinence from marriage and from meats, they are true neither to God nor man as God made him. A false religion grew up in the Middle Ages which taught, "You must get out of the world, deny sex, and cut yourself off from everything around." The stamp of false religion is that it denies that these sensibilities have any nobility in them. It is spiritual cowardice to deny these things because they have been made sordid and bestial; if they cannot be controlled for the glory of God, Jesus Christ has misled us. Remember that we have to live a Christian life in these bodies, to get the right alloy which will produce the thing Jesus Christ stood for. The Incarnation reveals the amalgam of the Divine and the human, the right alloy, that is, that which makes the Divine serviceable for current use.

One of the first ingredients for a man's thinking is that the Incarnation is a picture of what takes place in every man who is touched by the Spirit of God, that is, the Son of God is formed in him by regeneration. Jesus Christ's holiness has to do with human life as it is. It is not a mystical, aesthetic thing that cannot work in the ordinary things of life, it is a holiness that "can be achieved with an ordinary diet and a wife and five children."

(2) *Provident Discretions for Christians.*

The great danger of socialism is that it is vague, it has the right vision, but it ignores margins and expects to come to a bigger understanding of things while ignoring the facts that are. Or take sacerdotalism, which says the only way to build a governing peace over the human race is by an ecclesiastical system, such as the domination of the pope. We can see today how much mischief and uselessness underlies this teaching.

These things do not seem to be a way out, but remember they are. They give rest and sustaining and peace, but not on the best line. They crush instead of developing.

Another "way out" is the ultra-holiness line. There are those who go to the opposite extreme and say we must live a pure Divine life, ignoring all the claims of the natural. Jesus Christ taught that the natural must be sacrificed through obedience, and turned into the spiritual. If it is not, it will produce a tremendous divorce in the life.

(a) The Mischief of Absorption (Galatians 4:16-20). This teaching says: There are defects in the churches, but they are not to be swept away on that account, the defects must be corrected; form the churches into an imperial church which will dominate everything. That is what happened when Paul began to plant the Christian faith, the Judaisers came after him and said, "Now we must absorb this," and the same spirit is at work in ecclesiastical minds today. The only way to get peace, they say, is by a big church that will absorb everything; an imperial power to dominate. If you do, divisions will be quieted and a peace produced such as was produced by the Roman Empire, a peace that dominates by absorption.

The divisions of the churches are to be deplored, and denominationalism is to be deplored, but we must not forget that denominations have reared up the best men we know. The defects are clear and they have to be remedied; something will have to be done, and one suggested way out is this idea of absorption which has been proven in history to be a way out.

(b) The Mistiness of Abstractions (1 Corinthians 5:9-13). Socialism and false Christianity are both misty, they deal with the idea of absorption, that you have to run the purist line where it cannot be run, denying the fact of nations and of families as they really are. Paul says, "In your own spiritual relationships you have to be 'dead nuts' against sensuality, but don't be fanatical. You have to main-

tain your personal relationship in purity among those who are not pure, and see that no intermixture of impurity gets in. In your own spiritual community these things must not be." Our Lord takes the same line in Matthew 18:15-17.

Never attempt to solve outside problems first. If sin is to be destroyed in my personal life on the basis of redemption, it is to be destroyed outside me also; if sensuality is to be mortified in my personal life, it is to be mortified outside me also. The majority of us begin with the bigger problems outside and forget the one inside. A man has to learn the "plague of his own heart" before his own problems can be solved, then he will be free to help solve the problems outside.

The mistake is that we want to take the path of a shell. Jesus Christ says, "No, I have taken the long trail," and "in your patience possess you your souls," that is, acquire the new way of looking at things. There are problems not easy of solution, they need patient dealing with day in and day out. Take, for instance, the way some missionaries train converts with regard to marriage laws; they have tried the "hustling" dodge, and found it to be no good. It takes a long time to lift people to a cleaner "sty"; it is absurd to rush in a fine ethic of Christianity on people who have been living in polygamy, their education takes time. The danger of the visionaries is that they do not seem to know how to get their visions to walk, and they never will unless they remember and take into account these big facts of sex and money and food. Are you going to judge with the same standards a well brought up man with generations of good, clean blood in his veins, and a man who has generations of wrong and evil in his heredity? How are you going to judge the man who boils up with bestiality? It is with him not a matter of escaping from conventions, or of taking on the color of those he is with; there is the great fact underneath. You cannot judge him, you have to be immensely patient with him.

(c) *The Meaning of Affiliation (1 Peter 2:13-17).* In the present crisis another "way out" is not to ignore facts as they are, but to affiliate them; the ultimate end is that demarcations must go. It is the affiliation of churches, not the absorption of them, that will solve the problems, and the same with nations. But, remember, we are on crutches just now and there are things to be taken into account.

Every man is up against these things today—socialist or imperialist, he cannot think without being touched by problems. It is not that we can offer solutions for these problems, but that the line on which personal problems are solved by Jesus Christ is the line on which the bigger problems will be solved also. But it will take a long time, and we have need of patience. Answer the problem in yourself first: How long did it take you to get your ideas actual? to stand where you are now?

There are those in the national life who are visionaries and are apt to forget that at present we are not there, just as there are visionaries in the Christian life—I like the vision, but don't ask me how I am to make it real. I like orchids, but don't ask me to look at the miasmic swamp in which they grow; I like the fine flower of virtue, but don't show me how it was produced. No one is born virtuous, virtue and purity are the outcome of fight; innocence is natural. People have to have enough moral muscle in them to fight against the things that want to make them immoral; immediately they fight, they become virtuous in that particular. It is a difficult thing to fight for virtue. Virtue for a man, purity for a woman, and innocence for a child, is God's order.

In all our views we must get back to facts as they are. Keep your vision, but take facts as they are; make a clean sweep of the old rubbish, the creeds and notions, and then begin to build bit by bit. You will find that the personal problems are the ones that call first for solution, and when you have solved those, you can begin to help solve the others. If the men who get back after this war will remain true to what they saw in the agonies, they ought to begin to make the new impression felt along every line.

The Pressure of the Present

"The index to moral failure is to care more for a religious society than for the church, more for a trade union than for the nation" (Dr. Forsyth).

(1) Findings from the Historic Christ (Luke 11:17-26).
    (a) The Kingdom of God (v. 20).
    (b) The Kingdom of Satan (v. 18).
    (c) The Kingdom of Man (vv. 21-26).
"Christ ruined many careers and brought sorrow and death to many souls."

(2) Findings from Hysteric Christianity (Mark 9).
    (a) The Vision of God (v. 5).
    (b) The Valley of Godlessness (vv. 17-19).
    (c) The Verity of Gumption (v. 29).
"Don't throw on God the dirty work you are called to do."

A point of view is tyrannous, consequently when a man gets knocked about by circumstances and acquires other points of view, his findings are confused for a time.

We mean by "The Pressure of the Present" the things that crowd a man out from thinking on his own line. If he could only cut out the fact that he is a man, or that things are as they are, he could get on all right. We all have the trick of saying—If only I were not where I am!—If only I had not got the kind of people I have to live with! If our faith or our religion does not help us in the conditions we are in, we have either a further struggle to go through, or we had better abandon that faith and religion.

We have seen that there are ways out—the visionary way, the socialist way, or the mystical Christian way, each tending toward the brotherhood of man. The vision is all right, but how is it going to be made actual? It is easy to talk about God and holiness; humanity and love for one another; but present things must be taken into account. Jesus Christ's vision was unmistakable, and His demands from human beings were terrific, but He always took "things as they are" into account, and He insisted that in order to carry out His demands individuals must have the right "alloy." The Incarnation means the right alloy. For God to be of any use to human beings He must become incarnate; that means dust and deity mixed in one. If you have merely an abstraction, the vision without the dust of the actual, you will never make the vision real. As Dr. Forsyth points out, if in dealing with religious societies, you ignore the barriers and simply look forward to the time when there will be no barriers you are making a mistake and you will end in failure. The vision is right, but you must take things as they are into account. Our life as disciples is not a dream, but a discipline which calls for the use of all our powers.

There are two worlds—the actual and the real. My personal consciousness is at home in the actual world, but not in the real; it just touches the real, it touches God. There is an inference that there is a world other than the actual, but I am not at home in it; all I can get at by my personal consciousness is a fictitious reality. Neither the actual nor the ideal is the real; according to Jesus Christ the real can only be worked out on the line of personal experience. Our Lord was at home in the ideal as well as in the actual, and consequently everything in His personal life was real. We are apt to forget that in order to get at reality we have not only to use our heads, but our consciences. No one as yet has ever reached reality by his intellect. A person may have sublime views of life and at the same time be a moral tadpole in regard to actual life. The same with emotions; a person may have any number of aesthetic susceptibilities, the finest appreciation of color and feeling and sound, but in actual life prove that none of it touches the sordid actualities of life. There is only one thing in a human being that brings him to reality, and that is his conscience. Conscience is the faculty in me that fixes on the highest I know; and it is through conscience that man touches the reality of things and becomes transformed. It is then the intellect and the emotions can come together.

(1) Findings from the Historic Christ (Luke 11:17-26).

Christianity is not adherence to a set of principles—righteousness, goodness, uprightness—all these things are secondary. The first great fundamental thing about Christianity is a personal relationship to Jesus Christ that enables one to work out the ideal and actual as one in his own personal life.

No one thinks so clearly at any time or is ever so thrilled as in his teens. The tragedy begins when he finds that his actual life cannot be brought up to the standard of the ideal, and he closes with an agony of his own. Then he goes to preachers who talk about the ideal, or to books, thinking he will find the real thing; but too often he does not. He finds the vision there, but not working out in actual practice; and his agony deepens. The ideal presented by Jesus Christ fascinates some men right away; there is something enthralling about Him; but inevitably, sooner or later, they come to the experience of the early disciples, recorded in Mark 14:50: "They all forsook Him and fled." "I gave all I had to the ideal presented by Jesus Christ, I honestly tried my best to serve Him, but I cannot go on; the New Testament presents ideals beyond my attainment. I won't lower my ideals, although I realize that I can never hope to make them actual." No man is so labored or crushed as the man who, with the religion of ideals, finds he cannot carry them out. There are many more people in that attitude than is supposed. They are kept away from Jesus Christ by a sense of honesty as much as by dishonesty. "I don't deny that Jesus Christ saves—but if you only knew me!—the mistakes I have made, the wrong things I have done, the blundering things—I should be a perfect disgrace to Him." Our Lord says to such a one, "Come to Me . . . , and I will give you rest." When a man comes, he will realize that Jesus Christ does not tell him to do his best, but—Surrender to Me, and I will put into you that which will make the ideal and the actual one, and you will be able to work out in actual life what you see by the power of vision. Without Jesus Christ there is an unbridgeable gap between the ideal and the actual. The only way out is through a personal relationship to Him, a relationship with Himself whereby a man can transform the ideal and the actual into one and slowly work it out in his own experience, and then help other folks.

The thing you find to be the solution in your personal life is also the line of solution for other things. If Jesus Christ is the way for a person to make things real in his own life, He is also the way for things outside a man's personal life to be made real. It is easy to keep our intellects busy with the ideal, but the problem is how to bring the ideal and the actual together, how to make our actual life in accordance with our ideal. Jesus Christ says, "Unless one is born again, he cannot see the kingdom of God"; He is not talking about deliverance from hell, but about being born into a new realm. The religion of Jesus Christ means that a man is delivered from sin into something that makes him forget all about himself. The trick of pseudo-evangelism is that it drives a man into concentrated interest in himself. The curse of much modern religion is that it makes us desperately interested in ourselves, overweeningly concerned about our own whiteness.

These findings are not part and parcel of the average Christian conception of Jesus Christ, because we do not take our findings from the New Testament, we take them from what we have been taught about Jesus Christ. Jesus Christ said, "If I had not come and spoken to them, they would have no sin; but now they have no excuse for their sin" (John 15:22). Then why did He come? Why should He come with an ideal that knocks the bottom out of my self-realization? Why tell me to love my enemies when I hate them? Why tell me to be pure in heart when I am impure? Why should He taunt me with ideals? If Jesus Christ is only a teacher, then all He can do is to tantalize us, to erect a standard we cannot attain to; but when we are born gain of the Spirit of God, we know that He did not come only to teach us, He came to make us what He teaches we should be. These are some of the things that ought to be deduced from reading the New Testament.

(a) *The Kingdom of God (Luke 11:20)*. We know about the kingdom of man, but not about the other two kingdoms which belong to the domain Jesus Christ lived in.

The "strong man" is Satan; the "stronger than he," Jesus Christ. The result of Jesus Christ's coming is disturbance. "Think not that I am come to send peace on earth; I came not to send peace, but a sword" (Matthew 10:34). When Satan rules, his goods—the souls of men—are in peace; there is no breaking out into sin and wrongdoing, and before God can rule man's kingdom He must first overthrow this false rule. The coming of Jesus Christ is not a peaceful thing; it is overwhelming and frantically disturbing, because the first thing he does is to destroy every peace that is not based on a personal relationship to Himself. Am I willing to be born into the realm Jesus Christ is in? If I am, I must be prepared for chaos straight away in the realm I am in. The rule which has come in between God and man has to be eclipsed. Jesus Christ's entering into me means absolute chaos in the way I have been looking at things, a turning of everything upside down.

Just as Jesus Christ produces havoc in personal lives, so He will produce it all through on every line. For instance, if Jesus Christ had not obeyed the call of His Father, His own nation would not have blasphemed against the Holy Spirit. He ruined the career of a handful of fishermen, He disappointed and crushed the hopes of many and perturbed their peace. He continually produced havoc in people's lives.

(b) The Kingdom of Satan (Luke 11:18). According to the Bible the introduction of Satan is linked with man in his original unfallen state. In setting up the communication between them leading to the Fall, man was held responsible for yielding to the satanic pressure to sin in disobeying God, so reaping the diabolical consequences for all his human posterity (see Genesis 3:1-5; Romans 5:12).

Jesus Christ calls the self-realization point of view, "Satan," anti-Christ (Matthew 16:23). When our Lord comes face to face with Satan, He deals with him as representing the attitude we take up in organizing our lives apart from any consideration of God. For a thing to be satanic does not mean that it is an abominable and immoral thing.

The satanically managed man is moral, upright, proud, and individual; he is absolutely self-governed and has no need of God. Jesus Christ says, "What is highly esteemed among men is an abomination in the sight of God" (Luke 16:15).

(c) *The Kingdom of Man (Luke 11:21-26)*. Jesus Christ always said, "If any man will be My disciple"—He did not clamor for him or button-hole him. He never took a man off his guard, or use a revivalistic meeting to get a man out of his wits and then say, "Believe in me," but, "Take time and consider what you are doing; if you would be My disciple, you must lose your 'soul,'—your way of reasoning about things." When I am born from above, I have to reconstruct another soul, I have to look at things from a different standpoint—the standpoint of Jesus Christ. Jesus Christ taught non-resistance on the physical line so that people might resist more on the moral line. When He was brought face to face with evil, His attitude was "Get!"—no compromise.

When Jesus Christ comes in with His standards, a man's way of looking at things is upset, and he begins to see the point of view of Jesus Christ when he strikes his own personal agony. He is brought face to face with the possibility, that after all, Jesus Christ knows what He is talking about, and that rationalism may be a fools' paradise, and he himself an intellectual ostrich. We never blame our fundamental conception until we get deep enough down. Rationalism at the basis is wrong; it goes to pieces just where we expect it to prove right.

(2) *Findings from Hysteric Christianity, or Christianity based on sentimentality (Mark 9).*

(a) *The Vision of God (Mark 9:5)*. We are not built for mountains and dawns and artistic affinities; they are for moments of inspiration, that is all. We are built for the valley, for the ordinary stuff of life, and this is where we have to prove our mettle. A false Christianity takes us up on the mount and we want to stay there. But what about the demon-possessed world? Oh, let it go to hell! We are having a great time up here.

(b) *The Valley of Godlessness (Mark 9:17-19).* The intellectualist or dreamer who by his dreams or isolation is not made fitter to deal with actual life, proves that his dreams are mere hysterical drivel. If his dreams only succeed in making him hold aloof from his fellowmen, a visionary who deals only with things belonging to the mountain top, he is self-indulgent to a degree. No man has any right to be a spectator of his fellowmen; he ceases to be in touch with reality.

It is a great thing to be on the mount with God, and the mountains are meant for inspiration and meditation; but a man is taken there only in order that he may go down afterwards among the demon-possessed and lift them up. Our Christianity has been as powerless as dish water with regard to things as they are; consequently the net result of Christianity is judged to be a failure. But Christianity, according to Jesus Christ, has never been tried and failed; it has been tried and abandoned in individual cases because it has been found a bit too hard, too definite and emphatic, and for the same reason it has been abandoned in nations and in churches; but Christianity has never been tried and gone through with honorably and found to fail.

The same thing with regard to the socialistic vision; it is a great thing to have the vision, but those who have it are apt to forget the limitation of actual things as they are. Jesus Christ gives the vision of God, God's order; but He also gives us God's permissive will. God's order, according to Jesus Christ, is no sin, no sickness, no limitation, no evil, and no wrong: His permissive will allows these things, and I have to get at God's order through His permissive will by an effort of my own.

(c) *The Verity of Gumption (Mark 9:29).* The disciples had the stamp of all false hysteric religion. "You work a miracle; we don't want to accept the moral responsibility." Jesus Christ said, "You cannot do these things by magic, it must be done by concentration." Peter thought it would be a fine thing to remain on the mount, but Jesus Christ took them down and put them into the valley, that is, the place that explains the meaning of the vision. There are times when my false religion makes me want to throw my dirty work on God. Suppose I am a slovenly workman and get saved, and I say, "Well, I will ask God to make my work fine and clean"; He won't do it, it is not His job. God's job is to alter my heredity, I cannot alter that; but when my heredity is altered, I have to manifest my altered heredity in actual circumstances. This is not only true in personal life, but in every domain. For instance, God won't clear up our social conditions; Jesus Christ is not a social reformer, He came to alter us first, and if there is any social reform done on earth, we will have to do it. We are not to ask God to do what He has created us to do, any more than we are to attempt to do what He alone can do. Prayer is often a temptation to bank on a miracle of God instead of on a moral issue, that is, it is much easier to ask God to do my work than it is to do it myself. Until we are disciplined properly, we will always be inclined to bank on God's miracles and refuse to do the moral thing ourselves. It is our job, and it will never be done unless we do it.

Visions are great things, but it is useless to tell a man about a vision of God on earth unless you can get down into the mire he is in and lift him up; and the marvel is that if you have got hold of the vision of God and are working it out by moral obedience in your own life, you can do the lifting. Moral insight is gained only by obedience. The second I disobey in personal bodily chastity, I hinder everyone with whom I come in contact; if in moral integrity I disobey for one second, I hinder everyone; and if as a Christian I disobey in spiritual integrity, others will suffer too.

The vision must be worked out or there is no grip in it. The majority of us who are called Christians could do nothing when the war struck us. We had our visions of God and our notions of prayer, but we had no grip, we could not touch the demon-possessed. We have to deal with people who actually have done the wrong thing; can we lift them up into the place where they will become changed men? or can we only preach in a way that is equivalent to putting a snowdrift over a dung heap? If we cannot live in the demon-possessed valley, with the hold of God on us, lifting up those who are down by the power of the thing that is in us, our Christianity is only an abstraction.

We need to remember that the vision must be worked out in our own personal experience first. If the vision is real, the biggest test of it is that it makes God easier to believe in. Think of the men and women you know who have made it easier for you to believe in God. You go to them with your problems, and things get different, the atmosphere of your mind alters; you have come in contact with a man or woman who in his actual life is working out his vision. The best way you and I can help our fellowmen is to work out the thing in our own lives first. Unless it is backed up by our life, talking is of no use. We may talk a donkey's hind leg off, but we are powerless to do any lifting. If we look after the vision in our own life, we shall be a benediction to other people.

The Psychological Phase—I

> But I, amid the torture and the taunting,
>   I have had Thee!
> Thy hand was holding my hand fast and faster,
>   Thy voice was close to me;
> And glorious eyes said, "Follow Me, thy Master,
>   Smile as I smile thy faithfulness to see."

Divergent Fundamental Points

Health: A perfect balance between our organism and the outer world (Psalm 73:3-14).

Happiness: A perfect balance between our inclination and environment (Philippians 3:17-21).

Holiness: A perfect balance between our disposition and the law of God (John 14:27).

Socialism—Revelation 13:11-18
Spirituality—2 Corinthians 4:16-18
Superman—2 Thessalonians 2:3-12
Sanctification—1 Thessalonians 4:3; 5:23-24
Sin—1 John 3:8
Sacrament—1 John 3:3

The rationalist says, "I can explain the conscious by reason, therefore all the rest is reasonable." There are chaotic elements which burst up into a person's conscious life and make him know that there are things beyond reason; not that they contradict reason, but that they are different from it. The basis of things in an individual's personal life is tragedy; at any second there may come a terrific upheaval from underneath that may knock all his calculations to pieces. People may be good at dealing with problems on the outside but never have faced one inside their own breastbone. The thing that knocks the conceit out of a man is to get what Solomon talked about, a dose of "the plague of his own heart," he becomes a little less certain that he can rule himself. When I receive the Spirit of God, I am lifted not out of reason, but into touch with the infinite reason of God.

Health, happiness, and holiness are all divergent views as to what is the main aim of a man's life.

(1) *Health (Psalm 73:3-14).*

Health means the balance between my physical life and external nature, and is maintained purely by a sufficient fighting vitality within against things outside. Health is equilibrium maintained through a terrific power of fight. Disease means that the harmony of health is gone, and a sign that the fighting corpuscles are getting weak. The things which keep you going when you are alive, disintegrate you when you are dead. Everything that is not my physical life is designed to put me to death, but if I have enough fighting power I produce the balance of health.

The same is true in my moral life; everything that does not partake of the nature of virtue is the enemy of virtue in me, and it depends on what moral caliber I have as to whether I overcome and produce virtue. I am only moral if I have sufficient moral power in me to fight; immediately I fight, I am moral in that particular. Disinclination to sin is not virtue, any more than innocence is purity. Innocence has always to be shielded, purity is something that has been tested and tried and has triumphed, something that has character at the back of it, that can overcome, and has overcome. Virtue is acquired, and so is purity. Everything that is not virtuous tries to make me immoral. Always do something you don't need to do for the sake of doing it—it keeps you in moral fighting trim.

The same thing spiritually, everything that is not my spiritual life makes for its undoing. Holiness is the balance between my disposition and the laws of God as expressed in Jesus Christ, and if I have enough spiritual fighting capacity I shall produce a character that is like Jesus Christ's. Character must be attained, it is never given to us.

The basis of physical, moral, and spiritual life is antagonism.

"A healthy mind in a healthy body" is not always true, for some of the finest minds are in diseased bodies. On the other hand the psalmist talks about the "wicked"—"there are no pangs in their death : . . . They are not in trouble as other men, nor are they plagued like other men . . . Their eyes bulge with abundance; they have more than heart could wish." The healthy minded cult evades anything that would be likely to upset the health of the body.

A man can make certain forms of vice or drugs necessary to himself, and the moralist who ignores the fact that a man will suffer for a time by giving them up is nothing short of a fool. Every appetite I create demands satisfaction; and the harmony of my body depends on its being satisfied; but not the health of my moral life. If the moral life is allowed its way, the one who has maintained his bodily health by other means has to go to rack and ruin before he gets another balance. No wonder we will do anything to avoid conviction of sin! No one can have his state of mind altered without suffering for it in his body, and that is why we will do anything rather than be upset. "I like to listen to this talk about Jesus Christ, but don't put your finger on the thing that upsets my mind. Why should I bother with a standard of things that upsets me?"

The healthy minded cult runs through everything. If certain types of health are to be maintained, all social life will have to be re-faced, marriage will go by the board, and the higher amenities of friendship—all the best and noblest moral relationships.

Sin is a thing that puts man's self out of center altogether, making it ex-centric; and when the Spirit of God convicts him, the man knows he is wrongly related to God, to his own body, and to everything around him, and he is in a state of abject misery. The health of the body is upset, the balance pushed right out, by conviction of sin. Conviction of sin makes a man's beauty "to consume away like a moth." *Beauty* means the perfectly ordered completeness of man's whole nature. When once a person's mind is upset, that beauty begins to go, the equilibrium is upset. This accounts for the characteristic tendency abroad today: ignore sin, deny it ever was; if you make mistakes, forget them, live the healthy minded, open-hearted, sunshiny life, don't allow yourself to be convicted of sin.

To say "camp life has made men worse" is not true; nothing can! Camp life strips the veneer of civilized life from a man, and he comes out with what he is, he has to reveal himself, but nothing can make a man either better or worse than he is. In producing a splendid soldier you produce a splendid animal; then to be horrified because the animal gets its way is absurd. Is it our idea of a person's life that he should be a splendid healthy animal? If so, there are several things you will have to cut out; you will have to cut out Jesus Christ, never read the New Testament, don't let the standards of Jesus Christ—never hate, never lust, always do more than your duty—come in, or you will upset your health.

Health seems to be the basis of people's outlook, but it can never account for the problems.

Socialism (Revelation 13:11-18). Numbers are used as symbols for great big generalities, and the book of Revelation takes the number 666 to be the symbol of humanity sufficient for itself, it does not need God. The description given is of a great system in which humanity is its own god. (See Genesis 3:5, 22.) When the Bible talks of Man, it refers to the Federal Head of the race. The remarkable point of the vision is that it says the beast (in the spiritual, the self-realizing, sense) looks like a lamb, but talks like a dragon; that is, he looks like Jesus Christ, but when he talks, he talks like the old imperial dragon; when the crisis comes, he has tooth and claw exactly like the beast. The vision of socialism is magnificent; there are benedictions and blessings for mankind on the line of socialism which have never been yet; but if once the root is cut from redemption, it will be one of the most frantic forms of despotic tyranny the human race has ever known. It looks like the lamb, but when the big crisis comes, it gives life to the beast. It is in the wake of socialism that the resuscitation of Plato's ideas will come. Trace your ideas back to their roots, and you will find the root of socialism is in Plato's teaching. You will produce healthy organisms, but will you produce noble-minded men and women after the stamp of Jesus Christ?

(2) *Happiness (Philippians 3:17-21).*

There is a difference between environment and circumstances. Every man has his own environment; it is that element in his circumstances which fits his disposition. We each make our own environment, our personality does it for us. Happiness means we select only those things out of our circumstances that will keep us happy. It is the great basis of false Christianity. The Bible nowhere speaks about a "happy" Christian; it talks plentifully of joy. Happiness depends on things that happen, and may sometimes be an insult; joyfulness is never touched by external conditions, and a joyful heart is never an insult. Who could be happy these days? It would be the outcome of the most miserable selfishness to be happy under such conditions as are everywhere today, the sign of a shallow-minded, selfish individual. Happiness is the characteristic of a child's life, and God condemns us for taking happiness out of a child's life; but we should have done with happiness long ago, we should be men and women facing the stern issues of life, knowing that the grace of God is sufficient for every problem the devil can present.

We start with the idea that prosperity or happiness or morality is the end of a man's existence; according to God, it is something other than any of these, namely, "to glorify God and enjoy Him forever." Happiness would be all right if things were reasonable; it would be ideal if there were no self-interest, but every one of us is cunning enough to take advantage somewhere, and after a while my inclination is to get my happiness at your cost.

Superman (2 Thessalonians 2:3-12). In socialism there are things which look like Jesus Christ, but in the end they are more dragonlike than anything else, because one thing is evaded. The same with happiness, when once happiness and self-indulgence are allowed to rule and have their way, the end is the "Superman." If I believe I have the finest idea of happiness for my child, my child will have to come my way, and "damn the consequences." The same thing is true with a class or a nation or a state if it believes it is God. Each one of us in his own domain exhibits the tendency: in the state it is on a gigantic scale because the state is bigger than a man's individual life. The standard of happiness ends in the upset of happiness, in a tyranny and despotism of the most appalling order.

(3) Holiness (John 14:27).

Holiness is the balance between our disposition and the law of God as expressed in Jesus Christ, and it is such a stern thing that the majority of us have either not begun it, or we have begun it and left it alone.

What kind of peace had Jesus Christ? A peace that kept Him for thirty years at home with brothers and sisters who did not believe in Him; a peace that kept Him through three years of popularity, hatred, and scandal; and He says, "My peace I give to you . . . . Let not your heart be troubled," in other words, see that your heart does not get disturbed out of its relationship to Me.

But remember Jesus Christ has to upset the old equilibrium first. When a man is probed into by the Spirit of God, the waters of his conscious life get troubled and other ideas emerge. If I am going to follow the dictates of the Spirit of God and take up the attitude of Jesus Christ to things, it will produce an earthquake in my outlook. It will begin with the bodily life—"Do you not know that your body is the temple of the Holy Spirit?"

If you would be My disciple, says Jesus, that is the cost. No man can shift the center of his life without being upset. People of good taste are averse to the teaching of Jesus Christ, because if He is right, they are wrong. Take up any attitude of Jesus Christ's and let it work, and the first thing that happens is that the old order and the old peace go. You cannot get back peace on the same level. If once you have allowed Jesus Christ to upset the equilibrium, holiness is the inevitable result, or no peace for ever (Matthew 10:34).

If happiness or health is a person's main idea, let him keep away from Jesus Christ, for if he has any conscience at all, he will lose that health and happiness. Jesus Christ stands for holiness. At all costs a man must be rightly related to God. Redemption is the basis. When you take a point of view, watch the things it does not cover, and if you are going to think, think clean through, playing the man on every line.

(The latter part of the outline was not dealt with, so this chapter is necessarily incomplete.)

The Psychological Phase—II

Man becomes what he is.

For the glory and the passion of this midnight
I praise Thy name, I give Thee thanks, O Christ!
Thou that hast neither failed me nor forsaken
Through these hard hours with victory overpriced;
Now that I too of Thy passion have partaken,
For the world's sake—called—elected—sacrificed!

N. B.—On Personality and Individuality; Disposition and Character.

(1) Bias of Degeneration (Romans 5:12).
   (a) Disposition of Defiance (Romans 8:7).
   (b) Destiny of Death (Romans 6:23; 7:24; 8:6; 2 Corinthians 4:4).
   (c) Battle of the Margins (Hebrews 12:14-17).

(2) Bent of Regeneration (Galatians 1:15-16; 2:20).
   (a) Donation of Deity (1 Corinthians 1:30; Ephesians 2:5-6).
   (b) Disposition of Divinity (John 17:22; Philippians 2:5-8).
   (c) Borderland of the Mastery (Galatians 5:16-22).

Circumstances make a man reveal what spirit he is of. Crises reveal character more quickly than anything else.

Personality is of the nature of light, it can be merged; individuality is like a lamp which cannot merge. There may be many lamps, but only one light. Individuality cannot mix; it is all "elbows," it separates and isolates; it is the thing that characterizes us naturally, in our elementary condition we are all individual. Individuality is the shell, as it were, holding something more valuable than itself—the kernel, which is personality. The shell of individuality is God's created natural coating for the protection of the personal life. It preserves the personality, and is the characteristic of the child; but if I stick to my individuality and mistake it for the personal life, I shall remain isolated, a disintegrating force ending in destruction. Individuality counterfeits love. God designed human nature for Himself; individuality debases human nature for itself.

Personality merges, and you only get your real identity when you are merged with another person. A man has his individuality transfigured when he falls in love. When love or the Spirit of God strikes a man or woman, they are transformed, they no longer insist on their separate individuality. Christianity is personal, therefore it is un-individual. Personality is the characteristic of the spiritual man as individuality is the characteristic of the natural man. Our Lord never spoke in terms of individuality, of a man's "elbows" or isolated position, but in terms of personality, "that they all may be one." Our Lord can never be defined in terms of individuality or independence, but only in terms of personality. He was the antipodes of the individual; there was nothing independent or willful or self-assertive about Him. Jesus Christ emancipates the personality; the individuality is transfigured in the mastership of God's purpose in Christ Jesus, and the transfiguring element is love; personal, passionate devotion to Himself, and to others.

Disposition is the set of my mind; character is the whole trend of my life, not what I do occasionally. Character is what we make; disposition is what we are born with. We make our characters out of the disposition we have, and when we are born again we get a new disposition, the disposition of the Son of God. We cannot imitate the disposition of Jesus Christ; it is either there or it isn't. Our destiny is determined by our disposition; pre-ordination in regard to individual life depends entirely on the disposition of the individual. If the disposition of the Son of God is in me, then heaven and God are my destination; if the disposition in me is not the disposition of God, my home is as obviously certain with the devil. Our destiny is as eternal and as certain as God's throne; it is an unalterable decree of God; but I am free to choose by what disposition I am to be ruled. I cannot alter my disposition, but I can choose to let God alter it, and redemption means that in my practical experience Jesus Christ can give me a new heredity, a new disposition. Our destiny is something fixed by God, but determined by our disposition. We are all born with a disposition, that is, the peculiar bent of our personal life, and it is that which determines our destiny. Praying won't alter it, nor science, nor reasoning; if the destiny of a man is going to be altered it must be altered by the Creator (John 3:3).

We are much more than we are conscious of being. Our Lord said the Holy Spirit would bring back into our conscious mind the things He had said. We never forget a thing although often we cannot recall it; we hear it and it goes into the unconscious mind. Things go on in our unconscious minds that we know nothing about, and at any second they may burst up into our conscious life and perturb us. The Spirit of God enters into a person below the threshold of his consciousness. When He will emerge into the person's conscious mind no one can say; but when He does, there is an earthquake, and the man has to readjust his life in every particular. The Spirit of God entering into the spirit of man brings a totally new relationship to things.

(1) Bias of Degeneration (Romans 5:12).

There are only two men according to the Bible, Adam and Jesus Christ. They are the representatives of the human race. The "image of God" was male and female together in the way God created them (Genesis 5:1–2), and sin entered into the world by that "Man." The Bible does not say that God punished the human race for one man's sin, but that the disposition of sin, or, my claim to my right to myself, entered into the human race by one man. The disposition of sin is not immorality or wrongdoing, but my claim to my right to myself. When Jesus Christ faced people with all the forces of evil in them and people who were clean living, and moral, and upright, He did not pay any attention to the moral degradation of the one or to the moral attainment of the other; He was looking at something we do not see: at the disposition in both, not at the immorality or the morality, but at the disposition—my claim to my right to myself, self-realization, and He said: "If you would be My disciple, that must go."

(a) Disposition of Defiance (Romans 8:7). To say that "sin is nothing but the shadow of good" is not true. Evil, according to the Bible, is the shadow of good, but sin is positive defiance. You can be educated by evil, but not by sin. Sin is the positive disposition in me that has to be removed; evil is the negative thing outside me. There is no such thing as sin outside the Bible; sin is a revelation fact, and it is the one fact that accounts for the curious twist we find in things. We must take into account that there is a bias in

human nature—self-interest, self-realization; it may be refined or low, but it is there. Common sense says, what a wonderful being humankind is in the making! The New Testament says, what a magnificent ruin of what man was once! Which view covers the biggest number of facts?

The great element in sin is defiance against God. There is a difference between sin and sins; sin is a disposition and is never spoken of as being forgiven; sins are acts for which we are responsible. Sin is a thing we are born with, and we cannot touch sin; God touches sin in redemption. God never laid the sin of the human race on anybody but Himself, and in redemption He has dealt with the disposition of sin. A person cannot be forgiven for what he is not to blame, but God holds a person responsible for refusing to receive a new heredity when he sees that Jesus Christ can give it to him. In the Cross of Jesus Christ, God redeemed the whole human race from the possibility of damnation through the heredity of sin. If, when we realize that Jesus Christ came to deliver us from the wrong disposition by putting in a right one, we refuse to allow Him to do it, that is the moment when condemnation begins (John 3:19).

(b) *The Destiny of Death* (Romans 6:23; 7:24; 8:6; 2 Corinthians 4:4). Many a clean-living man is in the condition these verses describe. The domain Jesus Christ represents does not awaken a tremor of sympathy, something has to stab him wide awake, rouse him to other issues and bring him to his wits' end before the things Jesus Christ stands for are even interesting. You cannot make Jesus Christ mean anything to a person; He may be nothing to him one minute and everything the next; it depends on what happens. A man may go on well contented until something pierces his hide, or brings him up against the things which profoundly alter life; then suddenly he is within another frontier and it begins to be possible for him to see the kingdom in which Jesus Christ moves.

(c) Battle of the Margins (Hebrews 12:14-17). There is no effort about Esau, he is content with being once born; Jacob could not be satisfied with anything less than God. Jacob tried in a hundred and one ways, cunningly to satisfy himself, but it was of no use. Esau was a man who had no battles at all, or if he had any, he fought them all on the wrong side of the margins. A man is not brought up to the margins in an ordinary way, but only through an agony. We do not come near the margins until we are hit by a form of supreme suffering, and then we see we have been shutting our lives away from a great domain. If Jesus Christ is going to regenerate us, what is the problem He is up against? We have a heredity we had no say in, we are not holy, nor likely to be, Jesus Christ had the disposition of Deity, and He says we have to be fathomlessly pure in heart. If all He can do is to tell me that I must be holy, be what I never can be, present me with an ideal I cannot come anywhere near, His teaching plants despair; He is nothing more than a tantalizer and I wish He had never come. But if He is a Regenerator, One who first of all can put into me His own heredity, then I see what He is driving at in the Sermon on the Mount—that the disposition He puts in is like His own. There is not one characteristic in the Sermon on the Mount that fits in with a man's natural disposition; we may give our mental assent to it, but our actual life won't walk that road; Jesus Christ is the only one who can carry it out. Redemption means that Jesus Christ can put into anyone the hereditary disposition that was in Himself, and all the standards He gives are based on that disposition. Jesus Christ teaches that when His Spirit is in us, we shall manifest a likeness to Himself if we allow His disposition to react in us.

(2) Bent of Regeneration (Galatians 1:15-16; 2:20).

The heredity of the Son of God is planted in me by God, a moral miracle. Pseudo-evangelism has gone wildly off the track in that it has made salvation a bag of tricks whereby if I believe a certain shibboleth, I am tricked out of hell and made right for heaven—a travesty of the most tremendous revelation of the redemption of the human race by Jesus Christ. The New Testament's teaching about Christianity is that the Son of God is formed in me on the basis of His marvelous regeneration until, as Paul says, "the life I now live in the flesh"—not the life I am going to live when I get to heaven, but the life I now live in this flesh, the life that I see and know—"I live by faith of the Son of God who loved me, and gave Himself for me." What has happened to Paul? He has gone through his battle of the margins, he has gone through a moral decision with Jesus Christ, not an intellectual one; he has said—I agree with God in the things that He condemns in the Cross, self-interest, self-realization, though these have been dearer to me than my life; "I count all these things but loss for the excellency of the knowledge of Christ Jesus my Lord." It may take four minutes or forty years to be identified with Jesus Christ; it depends on whether I am willing to face the music, that is, forgo my hereditary right to my claim to myself and let Him take His claim to me. *Holy Spirit* is the name of the new disposition, and if Jesus Christ can put that into me (Luke 11:13), I see how things can happen.

(a) *Donation of Deity (1 Corinthians 1:30; Ephesians 2:5-6).* "The kingdom of God is within you" Jesus said, that is, without observation spirituality is a kingdom within, a new way of looking at things. The moral miracle of Christianity is that when I know my limitations, when I reach the frontiers by weakness not by will, Jesus Christ says, Blessed are you, I will do the rest. But I have to get there; it is not that God will not do anything for me until I do, but that he cannot. God cannot put into me, a moral being, the disposition that is in Jesus Christ unless I am conscious I need it. I cannot receive that which I do not believe I need; but when I am struck by an agony, or the sense of helplessness with regard to Jesus Christ's teaching, I am ready then to receive the donation of Deity.

In the natural world I am born with a heredity for which I am not responsible, and I have a disposition through that heredity; but I have not a character through heredity. God gives disposition, but never character. Habits are not transmitted by heredity, only tendencies and qualities; habits are formed by imitation. Heredity means that the qualities or defects of the parents are manifested in the children. If I receive the Spirit of God and become a son of God by right of regeneration, God does not give me my Christian character, I have to make that. He gives me the disposition of His Son; He puts the Holy Spirit into me, then He says— Now, breast and back as they should be, and work it out. My disposition tells through my body on to outward circumstance, and as I obey the Spirit of God and the word of God, I slowly form the Christian character.

(b) Disposition of Divinity (John 17:22; Philippians 2:5-8). The Spirit of Christ is given us, but not the mind of Christ. Every man is born with a human spirit, but he forms his own mind by the way his human spirit reacts in the circumstances he is in, and education gives power to a man to express his personal spirit better and better. The Spirit of Christ comes into me by regeneration, then I have to begin to form the mind of Christ, begin to look at things from a different standpoint—the standpoint of Jesus Christ, and to

do that I must lose my soul. Soul is not a thing I have got, soul is the way a man's personal spirit manifests itself in his body, the way he reasons about things, the rational expression of his personal spirit.

If my soul has been formed on the belief that rationalism is the basis of things, that things are calculable, then when the Spirit of God enters into my spirit and the principles of Jesus burst up into my life, the former foundations quake; I discover that tragedy, and not rationalism, is the basis of things, and I have to readjust my mind. When a person is saved by God's grace, it is the beginning of the end. Some are content to be dragged into salvation by the sheer mercy of God, but Jesus Christ's conception is that a person should become His disciple and begin to mold his thinking on the basis of the Spirit of God that comes into him. That takes time; when the crisis comes, am I going to obey the word the Spirit of God recalls to me?

(c) Borderland of Mastery (Galatians 5:16-22).

The Holy Spirit in a Christian wars against the old heredity; the new heredity and the old war one against another. Is that all God can do for me? destroy unity in life, make me a divided personality, and make me sick with conviction of sin? If that is all God can do, I would rather be an atheist; but if it is only a stage toward the borderland of mastery, that is a different matter. Paul says if I obey the Spirit of God, I must crucify the other mind. God cannot do that, I must do it myself. Yes, I will agree with the Spirit of God and go to the death of my old disposition (Romans 6:6). If I do not put to death the things in me that are not of God, they will put to death the things that are of God.

There are things in a man's natural life that are fine and beautiful, but when a man comes to Jesus Christ, he has to forgo them, and go to their "white funeral." This is a phrase

Tennyson uses in speaking of the "white funeral" of the single life; and that aspect is the only one that suits the spiritual life. Think of it in reference to babyhood: there comes a time when that phase dies and child life begins; there is a "white funeral" of the baby; and then a "white funeral" of the child and girlhood begins. Apply that spiritually. There is any amount in paganism that is good and virtuous, but if I am going on with Jesus Christ, I have to give those things a "white funeral," make a termination of them, and we very often get there through disenchantment. It is not true that everything in life apart from Christ is bad; there are many virtues that are good and moral, pride and self-interest are remarkably fine things in some aspects, "highly esteemed among men," but when I see Jesus Christ I have to go to their moral death. Any fool will give up wrongdoing and the devil, if he knows how to do it; but it takes a person in love with Jesus Christ to give up the best he has for Him. Jesus Christ does not demand that I give up the wrong, but the right, the best I have for him, namely, my right to myself. Will I agree to go through my "white funeral" and say I deliberately cut out my claim to my right to myself, deliberately go to the death of my self-will? If I will, instantly the Spirit of God begins to work, and slowly the new mind is formed.

These crises are reached in personal life, and we find the same thing in the life outside, and the only line of solution is this one. If we find a line of emancipation and solution for ourselves, we have also found a line of solution for problems outside ourselves. Moral problems are only solved by obedience. We cannot see what we see until we see it. Intellectually things can be worked out, but morally the solution is only reached by obedience. One step in obedience is worth years of study, and will take us into the center of

God's will for us. All our darkness comes because we will try to get into the thing head first. We must be born into the kingdom of God, Jesus says, before we can begin to think about it (John 3:3; 7:17), and when the life is there, we begin to form the masteries. We must take into account the bias of degeneration and the bent of regeneration, and our agreement with both is the only line on which we can solve the problems.

Humanity and Holiness

Past Error: A Christianity that utilized humanity.
Present Error: A humanity that utilizes Christianity.
Biblical point of view: God and man in union.

We are not suffering today from dogmatic theologians, but dogmatic scientists, socialists, and evolutionists. Today's cant is the cant of unspirituality (Dr. Forsyth).

> If your religion injures your intelligence, it is bad.
> If your religion injures your character, it is vicious.
> If your religion injures your conscience, it is criminal.
> (Amiel)

(1) *Body of Man—Solidarity of Sin (2 Thessalonians 2:3-4).*
    (a) Adam (Genesis 5:1-2)
    (b) Anarchy (Genesis 11:1-9).
    (c) Antichrist (1 John 4:3).

(2) *Body of Christ—Solidarity of Saints (1 Corinthians 12:12-27).*
    (a) Reconciliation (2 Corinthians 5:18-21).
    (b) Repentance (Acts 2:37-40).
    (c) Regeneration (1 Corinthians 12:12-27).

In the past the error of the Christian faith was that it paid no attention to the individual's actual life; it simply used human beings and made them catspaws for a religious line of things. The present error is that humanity utilizes Christianity; if Jesus Christ does not coincide with our line of things, we toss Him overboard; Humanity is on the throne. In the New Testament the point of view is God and Man in union.

(1) *Body of Man—Solidarity of Sin (2 Thessalonians 2:3-4).*

The New Testament way of looking at humanity is not the modern way. In the New Testament men and women exist, there is no such thing as "humanity," the human race as a whole.

A materialist says, "Because my religious beliefs do for me, therefore they are satisfactory." Not in the tiniest degree. The test of a man's religious faith is not that it does for him but that it will do for the worst wreck he ever knew. If every one were well brought up and had a fine heredity, then there are any number of intellectual forms of belief that would do. The materialistic line works like a searchlight, lighting up what it does and no more, but the daylight of actual experience reveals a hundred and one other facts. It does not show a clear simple path, but brings to light a multitude of facts never seen before. The evolutionist looks at human beings and says, What a glorious promise of what he is going to be! The New Testament looks at humankind's body and moral life and intelligence and says, What a ruin of what God designed him to be!

(a) Adam (Genesis 5:1-2). Adam was created to be the friend and companion of God; he was to have dominion over all the life in the air and earth and sea, but one thing he was not to have dominion over, and that was himself. Sin, according to the Bible, is man taking his right to himself, and

thereby he lost his lordship over the air and earth and sea. The only Being who ever walked this earth and was Lord of earth and air and sea as God designed man to be was Jesus Christ. Jesus Christ and Adam, as he was first created, are the normal men, the representatives of the human race. Jesus Christ mirrors what the human race will be like on the basis of redemption, a perfect oneness between God and man.

(b) *Anarchy (Genesis 11:1-9)*. This is the result in civilization of Adam's sin. Sin is red-handed anarchy against God. Not one in a thousand understands sin; we understand only about sins on the physical line, which are external weaknesses. In the common-sense domain sin does not amount to much; sin belongs to the real domain. The sin the Bible refers to is a terrific and powerful thing, a deliberate and emphatic independence of God and His claim to me, self-realization. Anarchy is the very nature of sin as the Bible reveals it. Other religions deal with sins; the Bible alone deals with sin. The first thing Jesus Christ faced in men was this heredity of sin, and it is because we have ignored it in our presentation of the gospel that the message of the gospel has lost its sting, its blasting power; we have drivelled it into insurance tickets for heaven, and made it deal only with the wastrel element of mankind. The average preaching of redemption deals mainly with the "scenic" cases. The message of Jesus Christ is different; He went straight to the disposition, and always said, "IF—you need not unless you like, but—IF any man will follow Me, let him give up his right to himself."

The Christian religion founds everything on the radical, positive nature of sin. Sin is self-realization, self-sufficiency, entire and complete mastership of myself—gain that, and you will lose control of everything over which God intended you to have dominion. Sin is not an act, but an hereditary disposition. Sin must be cleansed, and the revelation of redemption is that God through Jesus Christ has power to cleanse us from the heredity of sin. The curious thing is that we are blind to the fact of sin, and deal only with the effects of sin.

(c) Antichrist (1 John 4:3). Every spirit that dissolves Jesus by analysis is antichrist. What is the spirit that dissolves Him? My claim to my right to myself does it. Is Jesus Christ "boss" or am I? God's order is that He is to be absolute sovereign over me, and I am to be absolute sovereign over everything that is not God, and sin is the switch off, for the time being, that makes me my own "boss" and consequently "boss" of nothing else. I only gain the absolute control God intended me to have when I am brought back into perfect union with Him. If I want to know what the human race will be like on the basis of redemption, I shall find it mirrored in Jesus Christ, a perfect oneness between God and man, with no gap. In the meantime there is a gap. Sin, suffering, and the Book of God all bring a man to this realization, that there is something wrong at the basis of life, and that it cannot be put right by reason. If we make rationalism the basis of things, we shall find some great big tragedy will spit up and knock our theories to the winds. For instance, this war has taken our breath away and given all our findings a severe shaking. Before we seal up our mind on any of these matters, Jesus Christ says, "Believe also in Me."

Anything that puts self-realization on top is part of the solidarity of sin, which the Bible says will head up until it gets to the terrific and marvelous figure-head Paul refers to in 2 Thessalonians, revered and respected of every race and religion and nationality. The spirit in man, however religious, however sweet and delightful it may appear to men, if it is not the Spirit of God, must be "scattering" away from Jesus. "He who does not gather with Me scatters."

Christianity is based on another universe of facts than the universe we get at by our common sense; it is based on the universe of revelation facts which we only get at by faith born of the Spirit of God. The revelation which Christianity makes is that the essential nature of Deity is holiness, and the might of God is shown in that He became the weakest thing in His own creation. Jesus Christ claims that, on the basis of redemption, He has put the whole of the human race back to where God designed it to be, and individuals begin to see this when they are awakened by their own agony.

(2) *Body of Christ—Solidarity of Saints (1 Corinthians 12:12-27).*

The church of Jesus Christ is an organism; we are built up into Him, baptized by one Spirit into one body. Churchianity is an organization; Christianity is an organism. Organization is an enormous benefit until it is mistaken for the life. God has no concern about our organizations. When their purpose is finished He allows them to be swept aside, and if we are attached to the organization, we shall go with it. Organization is a great necessity, but not an end in itself, and to live for any organization is a spiritual disaster. Today we are hearing the crash of civilization and the crash of organizations everywhere.

Our word *church* is connected with civilized organizations of religious people; our Lord's attitude to the church is different. He says it is composed of those who have had a personal revelation from God as to who Jesus Christ is, and have made a public declaration of the same (Matthew 16:13-20).

The great conception today is not our being merged into God, but God being merged into us. The Christian line of things is that we are brought into union with God by love, not that we are absorbed into God. Jesus Christ maintains that this is to be brought about on the basis of His redemption alone. Mysticism says it can be brought about by a higher refinement of nature. The stupendous difference between the religion of Jesus Christ and every other religion under heaven is that His religion is one which brings help to the bottom of hell, not a religion that can deal only with what is fine and pure.

(a) *Reconciliation (2 Corinthians 5:18-21).* Sin is a fundamental relationship underneath; sin is not wrongdoing, it is wrong being, deliberate and emphatic independence of God. God, on the ground of redemption, has undertaken the responsibility for sin and for the removal of it, and Jesus Christ claims that he can plant in any of us His own heredity, which will remake us into the new order of humanity. If the human race apart from Jesus Christ is all right, then the redemption of Jesus Christ is a useless waste.

The revelation is not that Jesus Christ was punished for our sins, but that He was made to be sin. "Him who knew no sin" was made to be sin, that by His identification with it and removal of it, we might become what He was. Jesus Christ became identified not only with the disposition of sin, but with the very "body" of sin. He had not the disposition of sin in Himself, and no connection with the body of sin, but, "Him who knew no sin, He made to be sin." Jesus Christ went straight through identification with sin so that every man and woman on earth might be freed from sin by His atonement. He went through the depths of damnation and came out more than conqueror; consequently every one of us who is willing to be identified with Him is freed from the disposition of sin, freed from the connection with the body of sin, and can come out more than conqueror too because of what Jesus Christ has done. The revelation is not that Jesus Christ took on Him our fleshly sins—a man stands or falls by his own silly weaknesses—but that He took on Him the heredity of sin. God Himself became sin, and removed sin; no man can touch that. God made His own Son to be sin that He might make the sinner a saint. God Almighty took the problem of the sin of the world on His own shoulders, and it made Him stoop; He rehabilitated the whole human race; that is, He put the human race back to where He designed it to be, and any one of us in our actual conditions can enter into union with God on the ground of Jesus Christ's redemption. God has put the whole human race on the basis of redemption. A man cannot redeem himself; redemption is absolutely finished and complete; its reference to individual men is a question of their individual action.

(b) *Repentance (Acts 2:37-40).* There is a difference between a man altering his life, and repenting. A man may have lived a bad life, and suddenly stop being bad, not because he has repented, but because he is like an exhausted volcano; the fact that he has become good is no sign that he is a Christian. The bed-rock of Christianity is repentance. Repentance means that I estimate exactly what I am in God's sight, and I am sorry for it, and on the basis of redemption I become the opposite. The only repentant man is the holy man. Any man who knows himself knows that he cannot be holy, therefore if ever he is holy, it will be because God has "shipped" something into him, and he begins to bring forth the fruits of repentance. The disposition of the Son of God can only enter my life by the road of repentance. Strictly speaking, repentance is a gift of God; no man can repent when he chooses. A man can be remorseful when he chooses, but remorse is something less than repentance.

When God handles the wrong in a man it makes him turn to God and his life becomes a sacrament of experimental repentance.

(c) *Regeneration (1 Corinthians 12:12-27).* When I come to the end of myself and my self-sufficiency, in my destitution I can hear Jesus Christ say, Ask, and I will give you Holy Spirit. "Holy Spirit" is the experiential name for eternal life working in human beings here and now. Jesus Christ said, You have not that life in yourselves, and you cannot have it unless you get it through Me. He is referring to "Holy Spirit" life which by His resurrection He can impart. The Holy Spirit will take my spirit, soul and body and bring them back into communion with God, and lead me into identification with the death of Jesus Christ, until I know experientially that my old disposition, my right to myself is crucified with Him and my human nature is now free to obey the commands of God.

The doctrine of substitution is twofold. Not only is Jesus Christ identified with my sin, but I am identified with Him so that His ruling disposition is in me, and the moral transaction on my part is agreement with God's verdict on sin in the Cross of Jesus Christ. Redemption means that God through Jesus Christ can take the most miserable wreck and turn him into a son of God. As long as a man has his moral-ity well within his own grasp, Jesus Christ does not amount to anything to him, but when a man gets to his wits' end by agony and says involuntarily, "My God, what am I up against? There is something underneath I never knew was there," he begins to pay attention to what Jesus Christ says. A moral preparation is necessary before we can believe; truth is a moral vision and does not exist for a man until he sees it. There is a frontier outside which Jesus Christ does not tell; but when once we get over that frontier, He becomes all in all. God takes us through circumstances until we enter the moral frontiers where Jesus Christ tells.

When you come to your wits' end, remember there is a way out—personal relationship to God through the redemption of Jesus Christ.

> Oh, we're sunk enough here, God knows!
> But not quite so sunk that moments,
> Sure, though seldom, are denied us,
> When the spirit's true endowments
> Stand out plainly from its false ones,
> And apprise it if pursuing
> Or the right way or the wrong way,
> To its triumph or undoing.
>
> There are flashes struck from midnights,
> There are fire-flames noondays kindle,
> Whereby piled-up honors perish,
> Whereby swollen ambitions dwindle;
> While just this or that poor impulse,
> Which for once had play unstifled,
> Seems the sole work of a lifetime,
> That away the rest had trifled!

THE PILGRIM'S SONG BOOK

Psalm 120

We can judge a nation by its songs. The minor note is indicative of a crushed, but unconquered people. In the Bible there is nothing altogether minor; nothing, that is, of the nature of despair. The Bible deals with terrors and upsets, with people who have gotten into despair—in fact, the Bible deals with all that the devil can do, and yet all through there is the uncrushable certainty that in the end everything will be all right.

The songs of ascents are the autobiography of the children of God; they reveal their inner secrets. These psalms express not the outward, but the inward condition of the children of God, when they realize that they are pilgrims. We do not immediately realize that we are pilgrims; when a child is born into the world she is welcomed and for a time feels perfectly happy and at home. Neither when we are born again do we realize at once that we are pilgrims; rather, we feel more at home on the earth than ever; we have come into contact with the Creator of it all, and

> Heaven above is brighter blue,
> Earth around a sweeter green.

But as we go on, this sense of at-home-ness disappears and ultimately we realize a deep alienation to all that the world represents, and we recognize that we are "strangers and pilgrims on the earth," that "here we have no continuing city." That mood is represented in these psalms. God seems to delight to stir up our nests; it is not the devil who does it, but God; this is curiously unrecognized on our part.

The peace of this world can never be the peace of God. The peace of physical health, of mental healthy-mindedness, of prosperous circumstances, of civilization—not one of these is the peace of God, but the outcome of the souls of men being garrisoned by the prince of this world (see Luke 11:21). When we are born again from above and realize that we belong to God, we begin to recognize the element of destruction that there is imbedded in many of our Lord's words, for example, "Do not think that I came to bring peace on the earth. I did not come to bring peace but a sword." We realize that the reasoning of the world is not in accordance with the Bible, and we find we are alien to it.

Direction in Distress

"In my distress I cried to the LORD, and He heard me" (120:1).

If I am a child of God, distress will lead me to Him for direction. The distress comes not because I have done wrong, it is part of the inevitable result of not being at home in the world, of being in contact with those who reason and live from a different standpoint. We blunder when we try to make out that the prosperity referred to in the Old Testament is intended for us in this dispensation. Plainly that prosperity has never yet been fulfilled in the history of the world; it is going to be fulfilled, but it does not refer to this dispensation, which is the dispensation of the humiliation of the saints, not of their glorification. One of Satan's greatest delusions is to distract folks off on to the blessings that are merely secondary. We become sidetracked if we make physical health our aim and imagine that because we are children of God we shall always be perfectly well; that there will be great manifestations of God's power, thousands saved, and so on.

"In my distress . . ." There are elements in our circumstances if we are children of God that can only be described by the word *distress*; it would be untruthful to say it was otherwise. "Then will I go unto God," says the psalmist, not "with joy," but "unto God Who is my exceeding joy." We go to God when we have no joy in ourselves and find that His joy is our strength. Are our hearts resting in the certainty that God is full of joy although with us it is "clouds and darkness" because we are pilgrims?

"I cried to the LORD, and He heard me." It is one thing to cry to God and another thing to hear Him answer. We don't give God time to answer. We come in a great fuss and panic, but when all that is taken out of our hearts and we are silent before God, the quiet certainty comes—"I know God has heard me."

Deliverance from Deception

"*Deliver my soul, O LORD, from lying lips and from a deceitful tongue*" (120:2).

One of the hardest things on earth to bear is deception, especially when it comes through our friends. We do not need the grace of God to stand the deception or slander of an enemy, human pride will stand that; but to be wounded in the house of our friends takes us unawares. Judas had "lying lips"; we read that he kissed Jesus. Are we honest with our lips: It is only Christians who can be frank with one another, because their disposition has been altered by God (see Ephesians 4:29).

"*What shall be given to you, or what shall be done to you, you false tongue?*" (120:3).

Most of our relationships are carried on with discreet

deceit. The words "shrewdness," "diplomacy," "aye keep a bittie to yersel'," express an attitude essential in the life of the world, but a Christian has no time to be a dabster with his tongue, no time to profit by being clever. The teaching of the Sermon on the Mount is never to look for justice but never to cease to give it. We waste our time looking for justice; we have to see that we always give it to others. "If you are My disciple," Jesus says, "people won't play you fair; but never mind that, see that you play fair."

"*Sharp arrows of the warrior, with coals of the broom tree*" (120:4).

The Bible reveals the tongue to be the worst enemy a person has (see James 3:6-8)—Sharp arrows of the mighty— they never miss their mark. The same thing is true when we are born again: God sees that our words get home; but if we are not born again our words rankle and sting and annoy and spread destruction. Sarcasm is the weapon of a weak, spiteful nature, its literal meaning is to tear the flesh from the bone. The antipodes of sarcasm is irony—conveying your meaning by saying the opposite; irony is frequently used by the prophets.

Distraction For a Dwelling

"*Woe is me, that I dwell in Meshech, that I dwell among the tents of Kedar! My soul has dwelt too long with one who hates peace*" (120:5-6).

Our Lord lived for thirty years in that atmosphere (see John 7:5). We sing, "There's no place like home," but the author of that song was far away from home when he wrote it. The description the Bible gives of home is that it is a place of discipline. Naturally we do not like what God makes; we prefer our friends to our God-made relations. We are undressed morally in our home life and are apt to be meaner there than anywhere else. If we have been captious and mean with our relations, we will always exhibit that spirit until we become new creatures in Christ Jesus. That is why it is easier to go somewhere else, much easier often to go as a missionary than to stay at home. God alters the thing that matters.

In a Dilemma by the Disputers

"I am for peace; but when I speak, they are for war" (120:7).

There is nothing more terrible than for people to take what you say and to turn it into dispute (see Psalm 109:4). We are not to keep things back, but we realize that if we stand for God there will be the dilemma of dispute. "They say: What do they say? Let them say." Paul says the same thing: "But with me it is a very small thing that I should be judged by you or by a human court. In fact, I do not even judge myself" (1 Corinthians 4:3).

In a crisis we are always in danger of standing true to something that is acclaimed by this world rather than standing absolutely loyal to God. Had our Lord been a patriot, He would have been a traitor to His country in submitting to the Roman dominance; He ought to have led an insurrection—"This dominance is wrong. We must break it." Instead of that, He bowed His head to it. He submitted to the providential order of tyranny knowing that through it God was working out His purposes. "Do You not know that I have power to crucify You, and power to release You?" Jesus answered, "You could have no power at all against Me unless it had been given you from above." (John 19:10-11).

Note: No notes are available on Psalm 121.

Psalm 122

Gladness of Comradeship

"I was glad when they said to me, 'Let us go into the house of the LORD' " (122:1).

God begins with us individually in the experience of conscious salvation, then He unites us to one another. Notice the *altogetherness* of the saints all though the Epistles—"till we all come to the unity of the faith . . . to the measure of the stature of the fullness of Christ." None of us individually can reach the "fullness of Christ"; we reach that standard all together. "I have called you friends," said Jesus. The idea is that the presence of Jesus is the arena in which we live. A friend is one who makes me do my best.

Goings of a Community

"Our feet have been standing within your gates, O Jerusalem" (122:2).

The gifts of our ascended Lord—"apostles, prophets, evangelists"—are "for the equipping of the saints." If you should be in advance of the rest of the community, God will take you into "the ministry of the interior." Spiritual insight is not for the purpose of making us realize we are better than other people, but in order that our responsibility might be added to. If we neglect to go to God about our communities, our ministers, we become criticizing centers instead of ministers of the interior. God expects us to be intercessors, not dogmatic fault-finders, but vicarious intercessors, until other lives come up to the same standard. Locusts in their flight over a stream may drown by the million, but others keep coming until there is a way for the live ones to go over their bodies. God uses His saints in the same way. "The blood of the martyrs is the seed of the church." There are prominent names in the works of faith, such as Müller and Quarrier, but there are thousands of others whose names are not known. It is the same truth our Lord uttered regarding Himself, "Unless a grain of wheat falls into the ground and die, it remains alone; but if it dies it produces much fruit." The work in a community to begin with may be a wondrous delight, then it seems to die out, and if you do not know the teaching of our Lord you will say it is dead; it is not, it has fallen into the ground and died in its old form, but by and by it will bring forth fruit which will alter the whole landscape.

God's Own City

"*Jerusalem is built as a city that is compact together*" (122:3).

"He waited for the city which has foundations, whose builder and maker is God" (Hebrews 11:10).

"I, John, saw the holy city, New Jerusalem, coming down out of heaven from God, prepared as a bride adorned for her husband" (Revelation 21: 2).

What a curious anomaly—a city of God! We could have understood if it had been the *country* of God, but a holy *city* is inconceivable to us. The city of Jerusalem, like the temple, was ordained of God, that is why the children of Israel were so certain the prophets were wrong in saying that God would ever leave Jerusalem; but God did leave it, He left it desolate on account of the sins of the people.

There is a time coming when we shall live in God's own city; Abraham looked for it; John saw it, coming down out of heaven. Our present-day communities are man's attempt at building up the city of God; man is confident that if only God will give him time enough he will build not only a holy city, but a holy community and establish peace on earth, and God is allowing him ample opportunity to try, until he is satisfied that God's way is the only way.

Gathering of the Clans

"Where the tribes go up, the tribes of the LORD, *to the Testimony of Israel, to give thanks to the name of the* LORD*"* (122:4).

The prophets look forward to the time when all the tribes will meet together in harmony. It is a symbol of what happens in this dispensation of grace; there is absolute harmony in Christ Jesus, no matter what the difference of nationality may be. The Bible is the charter of the city of God, and all sorts and conditions of people have communion with one another through it. There is a gathering of the clans of all who belong to the race of the twice-born—"Now, therefore, you are no longer strangers and foreigners, but fellow citizens with the saints and members of the household of God." The saints find their closest unity in communion with God, but we have to be put through a great deal of discipline before the oneness for which Jesus prayed in John 17 is realized. You will find that God introduces you to teachers and friends who are just beyond you in attainment in order to keep you from stagnation.

Christ's Own Crown

"For thrones are set there for judgment, the thrones of the house of David" (122:5).

When the Lord stood before Pilate and he asked Him, "Are You a king then?" Jesus answered, "You say rightly that I am a King." "My kingdom is not of this world. If My kingdom were of this world, My servants would fight." The kingship of Jesus consists in the entire sanctification of individuals. "For Christ's Crown and Covenant" was the motto of the Scottish Covenanters. Am I eager to be saved and sanctified so that Jesus Christ is crowned King in my life? "You call Me Teacher and Lord; and you say well; for so I am"—but is He? Is He Lord and Master of our sentiments with regard to this war? of our passions and patriotic pride? We may think He is until we are brought into a crisis, and then we realize that there are whole domains over which He is not Lord and Master. This is true in individual life and in national life.

Generosity of Community

"*Pray for the peace of Jerusalem: 'May they prosper who love you'*" *(122:6).*

"Pray for the peace of the city" because it will be better for us as saints if the city is in peace. It is true that in times of war people are driven to God, but the distraction of war upsets the harmony and peace which are essential conditions for the worship of God. Are we set on praying for the peace of Jerusalem only because it will bring prosperity with God to souls?

Goodwill in Concentration

"*'Peace be within your walls, prosperity within your palaces.' For the sake of my brethren and companions, I will now say, 'Peace be within you'*" *(122:7-8).*

In times of prosperity we are apt to forget God. We imagine it does not matter whether we recognize Him or not. As long as we are comfortably clothed and fed and looked after, our civilization becomes an elaborate means of ignoring God.

"God bless Jerusalem"—for Jerusalem's sake? No, for my companions' sake. "God bless the world with peace"—because it is deserving of peace? No, because of the Christians in it. Because God's house is here, we pray "God bless Askrigg." Because of the saints in Britain, we pray "God bless Britain."

But remember God's blessing may mean God's blasting. If God is going to bless me, He must condemn and blast out of my being what he cannot bless. "Our God is a consuming fire." When we ask God to bless, we sometimes pray terrible havoc upon the things that are not of God. God will shake all that can be shaken, and He is doing it just now.

Graciousness in Compensation

"Because of the house of the LORD our God, I will seek your good" (122:9).

"Inasmuch as you did it to one of the least of these My brethren, you did it to Me." This is not the judgment of Christians, but of the nations who have never heard of Jesus. They are amazed at the magnanimity of His words—"Lord, when did we see you hungry and feed You?" If that is God's attitude to the nations who do not know Him, what is His attitude toward us? We are never told to walk in the light of conscience, but to walk in the light of the Lord. If Jesus Christ has taught me to be "As He is in this world," then in every particular in which I am not like Him, I shall be condemned. God engineers circumstances to see what we will do. Will we be the children of our Father in heaven, or will we go back again to the meaner, common-sense attitude? Will we stake all and stand true to Him? "Be faithful until death, and I will give you the crown of life." The crown of life means I shall see that my Lord has gotten the victory after all—even in me.

Psalm 123

This psalm represents the inner biography of faith. It is not easy to have faith in God, and it is not meant to be easy because we have to make character. God will shield us from no requirements of His sons and daughters any more than He shielded His own Son. It is an easy business to sit in an armchair and say, "Oh yes, I believe God will do this and that"; that is credulity, not faith. But let me say, "I believe God will supply all my needs," and then let me "run dry," no money, no outlook, and see whether I will go through the trial of my faith, or sink back and put my trust in something else. It is the trial of our faith that is precious. If we go through the trial, there is so much wealth laid up in our heavenly banking account to draw upon when the next test comes.

Direction of Aspiration

"*Unto You I lift up my eyes, O You who dwell in the heavens*" (123:1).

"*Unto You I lift up my eyes*"—we have to make the effort to look up. The things that make it difficult to look up are suffering, or difficulty, or murmuring. If you are suffering, it is intensely difficult to look up. The command to the Children of Israel when they were bitten by the fiery serpent was, "*Look* at the bronze serpent." We cannot look up if we are murmuring; we are like the child who does not want to do what he is told, and the father comes and says, "Now look up," but the child won't. We behave like that with God; our circumstances are hard, we are not making progress in life, and the Spirit of God says, "Look up," but we refuse and say, "I'm not going to play this game of faith any more." The counsel given by the writer to the Hebrews is based on the effort of the saint—*"let us lay aside every weight, . . ." "let us run with endurance the race that is set before us," "looking unto Jesus, . . ." "consider Him"* (12:1-3).

Description of the Attention

"*Behold, as the eyes of servants look to the hand of their masters, as the eyes of a maid to the hand of her mistress, so our eyes look to the* LORD *our God, until He have mercy on us*" (123:2).

God intends our attention to be arrested, He does not arrest it for us. The things Jesus tells us to consider are not things that compel our attention—"Consider the lilies of the field," "Look at the birds of the air." The Spirit of God instructs us to be attentive. Are our eyes so fixed upon God that we have spiritual discernment and can see His countenance in the dreadful cloud of war? Most of us are at our wits' end, we have no inkling of what God is doing because our eyes have not been waiting upon Him. We are apt to pay more attention to our newspaper than to God's Book, and spiritual leakage begins because we do not make the effort to lift up our eyes to God. "But we all, with unveiled face, beholding as in a mirror the glory of the Lord, are being transformed into the same image from glory to glory" (2 Corinthians 3:18). That is a description of entire reliance on God. Be careful of anything that is going to deflect your attention from God. It is easier to rely on God in big things than in little things. There is an enormous power in little things to distract our attention from God; that is why our Lord said that "the cares of this world," "the lusts of other things," would choke the word and make it unfruitful.

Distraction of Annoyance

"Have mercy on us, O LORD, have mercy on us! For we are exceedingly filled with contempt. Our soul is exceedingly filled with the scorning of those who are at ease, with the contempt of the proud" (123:3-4).

The thing to heed is not so much damage to our faith in God as damage to our temper of mind. "Therefore take heed to your spirit, that you do not deal treacherously" (Malachi 2:16). The temper of mind if it is not right with God is tremendous in its effects, it is the enemy that penetrates right into the soul and distracts us from God. There are certain tempers of mind we never dare indulge in; if we do, we find that they distract us from God, and until we get back into the quiet mood before God our faith in Him is nil, and our confidence in human ingenuity the thing that rules.

Spiritual leakage comes not so much through trouble on the outside as through imagining you have "screwed yourself a bit too high." For instance, you came to a particular crisis and made a conscientious stand for God and had the witness of the Spirit that everything was all right; but the weeks have gone by, and the months, and you are slowly beginning to come to the conclusion that you had been taking a stand a bit too high. Your friends come and say, "Now don't be a fool, you are only an ordinary human being; when you talked about this spiritual awakening we knew it was only a passing phase; you can't keep up the strain, God does not expect you to"; and you say, "Well, I suppose I was a bit too pretentious." It sounds wise and sensible, but the danger is that you do not rely on God any longer; reliance on worldly opinion has taken the place of reliance on God. We have to realize that no effort can be too high, because Jesus says we are to be the children of our Father in heaven. It must be my utmost for His highest all the time and every time.

"Have mercy upon us, O Lord, for we are exceedingly filled with contempt." As God's children we have to see that we keep looking in the face of God, otherwise we shall find our souls in the condition of being filled with contempt and annoyance, with the result that we are spiritually distracted instead of spiritually self-possessed. This is true in individual circumstances as well as national crises. It is not always the cross mood that leads to the cross speech, but the cross word that makes the cross mood. If in the morning you begin to talk crossly, before long you will *feel* desperately cross. Take to God the things that perturb your spirit. You notice that certain people are not going on spiritually and you begin to feel perturbed; if the discernment turns you to intercession, it is good; but if it turns to criticism it blocks you in your way to God. God never gives us discernment of what is wrong for us to criticize it, but that we might intercede.

"Unto You I lift up my eyes." The terrible thing is that we are likely to get to the place where we do not miss the consciousness of God's presence; we have gone on so long ignoring the lifting up of our eyes to Him that it has become the habit of our mind and it never bothers us. We go on depending on our own wits and ingenuity until suddenly God brings us to a halt and we realize how we have been losing out. Whenever there is spiritual leakage, remedy it immediately. It does not matter what you are doing, stop instantly when there is the realization that you are losing out before God; lift up your eyes to Him and tell Him you recognize it—"Lord, this thing has been coming in between my spirit and You, I am not resting in faith." Get it readjusted at once. There is always a suitable place to pray, to lift up your eyes to God; there is no need to get to a place of prayer, pray wherever you are. Confess before God that you have been distracted away from faith in Him; don't vindicate yourself. The lust of vindication is a state of mind that destroys the soul's faith in God—"I must explain myself"; "I must get people to understand." The remarkable thing about our Lord is that He never explained anything to anybody. Nothing ever distracted Him out of His oneness with God, and He prays, "that they may be one *just as We are one.*"

Psalm 124

Alternative Danger

" 'If it had not been the LORD who was on our side,' let Israel now say—" (124:1).

Facing an alternative is not to deal in supposition, but part of wisdom and understanding; supposition is wisdom gone to hysteria. In estimating the dangers which beset us we have to remember that they are not haphazard, but things that will happen. Our Lord told His disciples to lay their account with peril, with hatred, in fact He tells them to leap for joy "when men shall hate you, and when they shall separate you from their company, and shall reproach you and cast out your name as evil, for the Son of man's sake." (Luke 6:22-23). We are apt to look at this alternative as a supposition, but Jesus says it will happen and must be estimated. It is never wise to underestimate an enemy. We look upon the enemy of our souls as a conquered foe, so he is, but only to God, not to us.

(a) Estimate of Antagonism—"*If it had not been the LORD who was on our side, when men rose up against us, then they would have swallowed us alive, when their wrath was kindled against us*" (124:2-3).

We have to lay our account with the antagonism of men, it is a danger that is always with us. ". . . When *men* rose up against us"—not tendencies, not the moods of men, but men themselves. All that makes life either honorable or terrible is summed up in the word "men." In estimating the forces against us we are slow to believe in this antagonistic element, we look at them too haphazardly, not realizing that they are dead set against us. "But beware of men"—it is the last thing we do. The reason our Lord tells us to beware of men is that the human heart is "deceitful above all things, and desperately wicked," and if we put our trust in men we shall go under, because men are just like ourselves, and none of us in our wits before God would ever think of trusting ourselves; if we do it is a sign that we are ignorant of ourselves.

At heart people are antagonistic to the lordship of Jesus Christ. It is not antagonism to creeds or points of view, but antagonism encountered "for My name's sake." Many of us awaken antagonism by our way of stating things; we have to distinguish between being persecuted for some notion of our own and being persecuted "for My name's sake." We are apt to think only of the bad things as being against Jesus, but it is the refined things, the cultured things, the religious things that are dead against Jesus Christ unless they are loyal to Him. It was the religious people of our Lord's time who withstood Him, not the worldly. "If the world hates you, you know that it hated Me before it hated you" (John 15:18). These are the deliberate words of our Lord to His disciples. In the measure in which we are loyal to Jesus Christ the same thing happens to us; we are at a loss to understand why people should have the most apparently absurd antipathy to us. Their anger is strangely unaccountable; it is not irritation, but an inspired working against.

(b) Estimate of Agony—"*then the waters would have overwhelmed us, the stream would have gone over our soul*" (124:4).

One element in the alternative danger that attends the saints of God is the agony it produces. It is strange that God should make it that "through the shadow of an agony comes redemption"; strange that God's Son should be made perfect through suffering; strange that suffering should be one of the golden pathways for God's children. There are times in personal life when we are brought into an understanding of what Abraham experienced. "Get out of your country . . . ." It is not so much that we are misunderstood, but that suffering is brought on others through our being loyal to God, and it produces agony for which there is no relief on the human side, only on God's side. When we pray "Your kingdom come" we have to share in the pain of the world being born again; it is a desperate pain. God's servants are, as it were, the birth-throes of the new age. "My little children, for whom I labor in birth again until Christ is formed in you" (Galatians 4:19). Many of us receive the Holy Spirit, but immediately the throes begin we misunderstand God's purpose. We have to enter into the travail with Him until the world is born again. The world must be born again just as individuals are.

(c) Estimate of annihilation—*"then the swollen waters would have gone over our soul" (124:5).*

The ultimate result of the danger is annihilation, our Lord leaves us in no doubt about that; He always estimated things in the final analysis. Our Lord teaches that the forces against us work for our annihilation, "And you will be hated by all for My name's sake." Today we do not catch the drift of these words. It is not the question of a law of nature at work, but a law of antagonism, everything that is not loyal to Jesus Christ is against us. "Then Saul, still breathing threats and murder against the disciples of the Lord . . . ." Saul of Tarsus was spending all his educated manhood to annihilate those who were "of the Way." It is that spirit we have to estimate in the danger that besets us if we are true to God.

Appreciated Deliverance

"Blessed be the LORD, who has not given us as a prey to their teeth" (124:6).

The reason some of us are so tepid spiritually is that we do not realize that God has done anything for us. Many people are at work for God, not because they appreciate His salvation, but because they think they should be doing something for other people. Our Lord never called anyone to work for Him because they realize a need, but only on the basis on that He has done something for them. The only basis on which to work for God is an esteemed appreciation of His deliverance, that is, our personal history with God is so poignant that it constitutes our devotion to Him. God's deliverance makes us His absolute debtors. Have we taken into account what God has done for us? Estimate the alternative danger, and then begin to call on your soul to bless God for His deliverance. ". . . To whom little is forgiven, the same loves little."

(a) Entire Escape—"*Our soul has escaped as a bird from the snare of the fowlers; the snare is broken, and we have escaped*" (124:7).

God does not deliver us gradually, but suddenly, it is a perfect deliverance, a complete emancipation. When the deliverance is realized, it is realized altogether, from the crown of your head to the sole of our foot, and your devotion to God is on account of that deliverance. It is a good thing to begin prayer with praising God for His attributes, and for the way those attributes have been brought to bear on our personal salvation. Let your mind soak in the deliverance of God, and then praise Him for them.

(b) Eternal Element—"*Our help is in the name of the LORD who made heaven and earth*" (124:8).

Our help is not in what God has done, but in God

Himself. There is a danger of banking our faith and our testimony on our experience, whereas our experience is the gateway to a closer intimacy with God. Our help is in the name of the One who delivers. The dangers that beset us are real dangers, and if we estimate them we shall appreciate God's deliverance. Why our Lord said that self-pity was of the devil is that self-pity will prevent us appreciating God's deliverance. When we begin to say "Why has this happened to me?" "Why should this difficulty come, this upset?" it means that we are more concerned about getting our own way than in esteeming the marvelous deliverance God has wrought. We read of God's people of old that "they soon forgot His works . . .", and we are in danger of doing the same unless we continually lift up our eyes to God and bless Him for His deliverances.

Psalm 125

The Fastnesses of the Godly

"Those who trust in the LORD are like Mount Zion, which cannot be moved, but abides forever" (125:1).

The security of the eternal God is what we are to have confidence in, and the psalmist likens that security to the mountains, because a mountain is the most stable thing we know. There is nothing so secure as the salvation of God; it is as eternal as the mountains, and it is our trust in God that brings us the conscious realization of this. The one thing Satan tries to shake is our confidence in God. It is not difficult for our confidence to be shaken if we build on our experience; but if we realize that all we experience is but the doorway leading to the knowledge of God, Satan may shake that as much as he likes, but he cannot shake the fact that God remains faithful (see Timothy 2:13), and we must not cast away our confidence in Him. It is not our trust that keeps us, but the God in whom we trust who keeps us. We are always in danger of trusting in our trust, believing our belief, having faith in our faith. All these things can be shaken; we have to base our faith on those things which cannot be shaken (Hebrews 12:27).

Our consciousness of God is meant to introduce us to God, not to our experience of Him. Jesus said, ". . . no man is able to snatch them out of My Father's hand" (John 10:29). No power, however mighty, is able to pluck us out of the hand of God, so long as that power is outside us. Our Lord did not say, however, that His sheep had not power to take themselves out. The devil cannot take us out, neither can the enemy, saving our own willfulness. God does not destroy our personal power to disobey Him; if He did, we would become mechanical and useless. No power outside, from the devil downward, can take us out of God's hand; so long as we remain faithful, we are as eternally secure as God Himself.

The Frontiers of God

"As the mountains surround Jerusalem, so the LORD *surrounds His people from this time forth and forever" (125:2).*

There are margins beyond which the Spirit of God does not work. Nightingales will not sing outside certain geographical areas, and that is an exact illustration of the frontiers of God. There is a place where God reveals His face, and that place has moral frontiers, not physical. We can blind our minds by perverse thinking; blind our moral life by crooked dealing in business, or by sin. We can never get away from God geographically, but we can get away from Him morally. The writer to the Hebrews mentions the moral frontier, "Let your conduct be without covetousness; be content with such things as you have" (13:5). Outside that moral frontier, God does not reveal His face. Let me become impatient, let me fix my heart on gain, and I do not see God. If I enthrone anything other than God in my life, God retires and lets the other god do what it can. The majority of us do not enthrone God, we enthrone commonsense. We make our decisions and then ask the real God to bless our god's decision. We say, "It is common sense to do this thing," and God leaves us, because we are outside the frontier where He works. "Keep yourself from the love of money, and be content." Think of the imperative haste in our spirit to wish we were somewhere else! That danger is always there, and we have to watch it. When I wish I were somewhere else I am not doing my duty to God where I am. I am wool-gathering, fooling with my own soul; if I am God's child I have no business to be distracted. If I keep myself from covetousness, content with the things I have, I remain within the frontiers of God. If I have the spirit of covetousness in my heart I have no right to say, "The Lord is my helper"—He is not, He is my destroyer. I have no right to say I am content and yet have a mood that is not contented. If I am ill-tempered, set on some change of circumstances, I find God is not supporting me at all; I have worried myself outside the moral frontier where He works and my soul won't sing; there is no joy in God, no peace in believing. We have to watch that we are not enticed outside the frontier of our own control, just as soldiers have to watch. If they get outside the frontier of their strategy they will probably be killed, and so we have to watch that we are not enticed outside God's frontier. Remember, no man can take us outside, it is our own stupidity that takes us out. When we realize that we have got outside the moral frontier, the only thing to do is to get back again and realize what the apostle Paul says in Philippians 4:11-13.

The Faithfulness of Godliness

"For the scepter of wickedness shall not rest on the land allotted to the righteous, lest the righteous reach out their hands to iniquity" (125:3).

The rod means two things—it is used to count the sheep, and it is used to destroy the wild beast that suddenly springs out on the sheep (see Psalm 23:4). The man of sin will have his rod, he will do clever tricks, he will put the mark of the beast on every business system that he sanctions, and those who do not have that mark on them can never do business under the regime of the man of sin. Suppose that you find that the people who are "counted in" under the mark of the beast succeed, and you do not succeed, you may be tempted to negotiate the thing and say, "Well, I don't know, if I did this thing it would save me; I had better just compromise a bit." We must never do that. "The rod of the wicked shall not rest on the righteous," God says. There is no need to fear, if we keep within the moral frontiers of God we can say boldly, "The Lord is my helper." We do not need to mind how the wicked bluster and say, "If you don't do this and that, you will starve." Be faithful, make holiness your aim, holiness in every relationship—money, food, clothes, friendship—then you will see the Lord in all these domains.

The Fitness of Goodness

"*Do good, O* LORD, *to those who are good, and to those who are upright in their hearts*" *(125:4).*

Our Lord warned the disciples that they would be put out of the synagogue, and be killed (see John 16:2), but He says, "Don't mind about that, beware only of not doing your duty according to My commandments, because that will destroy both soul and body in hell." (See Matthew 10:28; Revelation 2:10). We are apt to make salvation mean the saving of our skin. The death of our body, the sudden breaking-up of the house of life, may be the salvation of our soul. In times of peace "honesty may be the best policy," but if we work on the idea that it is better physically and prosperously to be good, that is the wrong motive; the right motive is devotion to God, remaining absolutely true to God, no matter what it costs.

The Futility of Godlessness

"*As for such as turn aside to their crooked ways, the* LORD *shall lead them away with the workers of iniquity*" *(125:5).*

There is no reference in the Bible to natural law. We talk of certain things as the inevitable result of what a man does: the Bible says, God. The psalmist says, "The Lord shall lead them away." God is active in every relationship; it is not natural law or mathematical logic, but God working all through. No man has a fate portioned out to him; a man's disposition makes what people call his fate. The course of deliberately remaining independent of God ends in damnation, by God's direct decree, not as an inevitable happening; and the course of dependence upon God ends in heaven, by God's decree, not by chance. Either course has God behind it. It is the glorious risk of the Christian life. The apostle Peter gives the warning, "Beware lest you also fall from your own steadfastness" (2 Peter 3:17). God does not save us from facing the music, or shelter us from any of the requirements of sons and daughters (see John 4:4). As long as we remain within the moral frontiers of God, watching our hearts lest we give way to ill-content, to covetousness, or self-pity, the things which take us outside God's frontier, then God says, "I will in no way fail you, neither will I in any way forsake you."

Psalm 126

The Emotion of Deliverance
"When the LORD brought back the captivity of Zion, we were like those who dream" (126:1).

Religion is never intellectual, it is always passionate and emotional; but the curious thing is that it is religion that leads to emotion, not emotion to religion. If religion does not make for passion and emotion, it is not the true kind. When you realize that you are saved, that God has forgiven your sins, given you the Holy Spirit, I defy you not to be carried away with emotion. Religion which makes for logic and reason is not religion, but to try to make religion out of emotion is to take a false step. Our Lord bases everything on life as it is, and life is implicit. For instance, you cannot explicitly state what love is, but love is the implicit thing that makes life worth living. You cannot explicitly state what sin is, but sin is the implicit thing that curses life. You cannot explicitly state what death is, all the scientific jargon in the world cannot define death; death is the implicit thing which destroys life as we know it. A child is a good illustration of the implicit, you cannot imagine a child without emotion, always logical, reasonable, and well-balanced, he would not be a child but a prig.

Emotion is not simply an overplus of feeling, it is life lived at white-heat, a state of wonder. To lose wonder is to lose the true element of religion. Has the sense of wonder been dying down in your religious life? If so, you need to get back to the Source. If you have lost the fervor of delight in God, tell Him so. The old divines used to ask God for the grace of trembling, that is, the sense of wonder. When wonder goes out of natural love, something or someone is to be severely blamed; wonder ought never to go. With a child the element of wonder is always there, a freshness and spontaneity, and the same is true of those who follow Jesus Christ's teaching and become as little children.

People have the idea that Christianity and Stoicism are alike; the writings of the stoics sound so like the teaching of Jesus Christ, but just at the point where they seem most alike, they are most divergent. A stoic overcomes the world by making himself indifferent, by passionlessness; the saint overcomes the world by passionateness, by the passion of his love for Jesus Christ.

The Excitement of Delight

"Then our mouth was filled with laughter, and our tongue with singing. Then they said among the nations, 'The LORD has done great things for them'" (126:2).

They were carried completely off their feet with amazement and delight over what God had done (see Genesis 17:17; Isaiah 60:5). A person will say, "I do not doubt that God can forgive sin, that He can give the Holy Spirit and make men holy, but it cannot possibly mean me! When I come before God I remember all my blunders and sins." When he realizes that it does mean him, then comes this moral hysteria—"It is too good to be true!" With God a thing is never too good to be true; it is too good not to be true.

Ruskin says that early in life he could never see a hedgerow without emotion, then later on, when problems of heart and life were busy with him, he saw nothing in nature; but as soon as the inner turmoil was settled, not only did he get the old joy back, but a redoubled joy. If we have no delight in God, it is because we are too far away from the childlike relationship to Him. If there is an internal struggle on, get it put right and you will experience delight in Him.

The Ecstasy of His Doings

"*The LORD has done great things for us; and we are glad. Bring back our captivity, O LORD, as the streams in the South*" (126:3-4).

Whenever God brings His deliverances they are so supernatural that we are staggered with amazement. It is one of the most helpful spiritual exercises to reckon what God has done for us already. When God wanted to make His ancient people realize what manner of God He was, He said, "Remember the crossing of the Red Sea," and in the New Testament Paul says, "Remember, it is God who raised Jesus from the dead. . . ." These two things are the unit of measurement of God's power. If I want to know what God can do, He is the God Who made a way through the sea; if it is a question of power for my life, the measurement of that is the resurrection of Jesus.

"Bring back our captivity, O LORD, . . ." I call upon my soul to remember what God has done and it makes me bold to entreat Him to do it again. It is a crime to give way to self-pity, to be weak in God's strength when all this God is ours. We have to "build ourselves up on our most holy faith." Robert Louis Stevenson asked God to forgive him if he had "shown no morning face"; and Dante places in the lowest circles of Hell those who have been gloomy in the summer air.

The Enlightenment of Drudgery

"*Those who sow in tears shall reap in joy. He who continually goes forth weeping, bearing seed for sowing, shall doubt-*

less come again with rejoicing, bringing his sheaves with him" (126:5-6).

We make the blunder of wanting to sow and plough and reap all at the same time. We forget what our Lord said, that "one sows, and another reaps." "Those who sow in tears . . ."—it looks as if the seed were drowned. You can see that seed when it is in the basket, but when it falls into the ground, it disappears (see John 12:24). The same thing is true with regard to Sunday school work or meetings, it looks as if everything were flung away, you cannot see anything happening; but the seed is there. "Those who sow in tears *shall reap in joy.*" "Cast your bread upon the waters, for you will find it after many days." The seed is the word of God, and no word of God is ever fruitless. If I know that the sowing is going to bring forth fruit, I am blessed in the drudgery. Drudgery is never blessed, but drudgery can be enlightened." The psalmist says, "You have enlarged me in distress"; the enlargement comes through knowing that God is looking after everything. Before, when I came to a difficult bit of the way I was staggered, but now through the affliction and suffering I can put my foot down more firmly (see Romans 8:35-39).

Psalm 127

Direction by Countenancing God

"Unless the LORD builds the house, they labor in vain who build it: unless the LORD guards the city, the watchman stays awake in vain" (127:1).

"Instead you ought to say, 'If the Lord wills, we shall live and do this or that' " (see James 4:13-15).

Do I countenance God like that? not have my face towards Him, but my whole person directed by that dominating thought? One of the greatest evidences that we are born again of God is that we perceive the kingdom of God. When I am born from above I countenance God; the arm of the Lord is revealed and I see God as the Architect, as the One who is doing all things. God is never away off somewhere else; He is always there. It is this fact that needs to be taken into consideration. Do I countenance the fact that God is engineering my bodily life and all that I come in contact with? I mention the body because that is the physical case in which our spirit works. If I do not countenance God in that, my faith is jargon. If I enthrone common sense as God, there are great regions of my life in which I do not countenance God.

"Unless the LORD builds the house . . .", the house of the mind or heart. God is building us for Himself, not for ourselves. Do I realize that my body is the temple of the Holy Spirit, or am I educating myself for myself? If I have an ambition, just where that ambition rules I do not countenance God, I cannot, because my ambition rules and I won't allow

God to thwart it. If I do not countenance God in every relationship of my life I shall end in disaster. We get the life of God all at once, but we do not learn to obey all at once; we only learn to obey by the discipline of life.

Distracted Man

"It is vain for you that you rise up early, to sit up late, to eat the bread of sorrows; for so He gives His beloved sleep" (127:2).

This verse describes an amateur providence. We are all amateur providences, until we learn better, we are most impertinent toward God, we tell Him there are certain things we will never allow to happen in other lives, and God comes and says, "Don't interfere with that life any more." Are you "rising up early" and "sitting up late" to try and unravel difficulties? You cannot do it. It is a great thing to get to the place where you countenance God and know He rules. It is not done by impulse, but by a settled and abiding conviction based on God's truth and the discipline of life. I know that God rules; and He gives me power to perceive His rule. There is no use sitting up late or rising up early, I must do the work that lies before me, and avoid worry as I would the devil. "It is vain for you to rise up early, to sit up late . . ." If I take time from sleep, God's punishment rests on me; or if I take time in sleep when I should be working, He punishes me. Sloth is as bad as being a fussy workman in God's sight. We have no business to be distracted.

I wonder if we have ever considered the biblical implications about sleep? It is not true to say that sleep is simply meant for physical recuperation; surely much less time than God has ordered would have served that purpose. The psalmist suggests a deep, profound ministry for sleep—more than mere physical recuperation. "For so He gives His beloved [in] sleep." The deepest concerns of our souls, whether they be good or bad, are furthered during sleep. It is not merely a physical fact that you go to bed perplexed and wake clear-minded; God has been ministering to you during sleep. Sometimes God cannot get at us until we are asleep. In the Bible there are times when in the deep slumber of the body God has taken the souls of His servants into deeper communion with Himself (see Genesis 2:21; 15:12). Often when a problem or perplexity harasses the mind and there seems no solution, after a night's rest you find the solution easy, and the problem has no further perplexity. Think of the security of the saint in sleeping or in waking, "You shall not be afraid of the terror by night, nor of the arrow that flies by day." Sleep is God's celestial nurse who croons away our consciousness, and God deals with the unconscious life of the soul in places where only He and His angels have charge. As you retire to rest, give your soul and God a time together, and commit your life to God with a conscious peace for the hours of sleep, and deep and profound developments will go on in spirit, soul, and body by the kind creating hand of our God.

Disregarded Munificence

"Behold, children are a heritage from the LORD, *the fruit of the womb is a reward. Like arrows in the hand of a warrior, so are the children of one's youth" (127:3-4).*

Things go by threes in the Bible: Father, Son, and Holy Spirit; God, Church, converts; husband, wife, children. It is God's order, not man's. Whenever one of the three is missing, there is something wrong. If you have a house, the next thing the Bible counsels is hospitality—"given to [pursuing] hospitality" (Romans 12:13); give your whole mind to it. "Do not forget to entertain strangers, for by so doing some have unwittingly entertained angels" (Hebrews 13:2). That is the way the blessing comes. When we begin to try to economize, God puts dry rot in us instantly. I don't care what line the economy takes, it produces dry rot. When we have the lavish hand, there is munificence at once. "There is one who scatters, yet increases more; and there is one who withholds more than is right, but it leads to poverty" (Proverbs 11:24). It is the "third" element being recognized. Have I got three factors in my thinking, or only two? Is it God and myself? Then I am wrong. It is God and myself for God's purposes. Do I want to be saved that I may be right with God, or that God may get His purpose through me?

Delivering Maneuvers

"*Happy is the man who has his quiver full of them: they shall not be ashamed, but shall speak with their enemies in the gate*" (127:5).

It is the element of the "third" that makes a man wealthy. ". . . trained servants who were born in his own house" (Genesis 14:14). Have I been able to reproduce my own kind spiritually? If so, in a time of difficulty I will be brought through magnificently victorious; but woe be to the spiritual man who has never produced his own kind, when the difficulties come there is none to assist, he is isolated and lonely. It is the production of the "third" that returns to you in victory. When we are right with God, Jesus says, "out of his heart will flow rivers of living water." Immediately you are in difficulties a thousand and one come to assist in prayer; they face the enemy in the gates. That is the great basal truth of the League of Prayer, the clustering together of the children of God. It is those who have been the means of blessing who keep you from the onslaughts of the enemy. We shall be amazed to find how much we are indebted to people we never think about, simply because they were introduced to God through us, and in our difficulties they come to our aid. There is the wire of communication when the maneuvers take place, and we are happily delivered. The kingdoms of this world are founded on strong individuals, consequently they go. Jesus Christ founds His kingdom on the weakest link, a baby. God made His own Son a babe. We must base our thinking on the rugged facts of life according to God's Book, and not according to the finesse of modern civilization. Let us not be so careful as to how we offend or please human ears, but let us never offend God's ears.

Psalm 128

Seemliness of Sanctity

"Blessed is every one who fears the LORD, who walks in His ways" (128:1).

The remarkable thing about fearing God is that when you fear God you fear nothing else, whereas if you do not fear God you fear everything else. "Blessed is every one who fears the LORD." The writer to the Hebrews tells us to fear lest haply there should be any promise of God's of which we come short (4:1). Are we alert enough along this line? ". . . who walk in His ways." The word *walk* breathes character, it is the symbol for seemly behavior. John "saw Jesus [walking]"—not in a moment of ecstasy and transfiguration but "[walking] toward him, and said, 'Behold! The Lamb of God!' " "Walk worthy," says the apostle Paul, worthy, that is, toward God, not toward man, because man's standards are not God's. When a man says he is sanctified, the charge is often made, and there is no reply to it, "Remember, you are not perfect." A saint is required to be perfect toward God. "*Walk before Me*, and be blameless"; the standard of judgment is not man's standard, but God's. Our conduct before men will be judged by whether we walk in the seemliness of sanctity before God. That means conduct, according to the highest we know, and the striking thing is that the highest we know is God Himself. "Therefore you shall be perfect, just as your Father in heaven is perfect."

There is something in human nature that enables it to go through a big crisis, but we do need help from God to walk worthily the sixty seconds of every minute. Am I behaving myself in God's sight in the seemliness of sanctity to those who are nearest to me? in my letter-writing? in my study? Is the one great lodestar of my life "walking in His ways"? The thing we have to guard against is wanting to be somewhere else. Have I sufficient of the grace of God to behave myself as His child where I am? It is one thing to feel the sufficiency of God in a prayer meeting and in times of delight and excitement, but another thing to realize His sufficiency in whatever setting we may be—in a thunderstorm or on a calm summer day, in a cottage or a college, in an antique shop or on a moor.

Satisfaction in Strenuousness

"When you eat the labor of your hands, you shall be happy, and it shall be well with you" (128:2).

This verse reveals the connection between the natural creation and the regenerated creation. We have to be awake strenuously to the fact that our body is the temple of the Holy Spirit, not only in the spiritual sense, but in the physical sense. When we are born from above we are apt to despise the clay of which we are made. The natural creation and the creation of grace work together, and what we are apt to call the sordid things, laboring with our hands, and eating and drinking, have to be turned into spiritual exercises by obedience, then we shall "eat and drink, and do all to the glory of God." There must be a uniting in personal experience of the two creations. It cannot be done all at once, there are whole tracts of life which have to be disciplined. "Your body is the temple of the Holy Spirit," it is the handiwork of God and it is in these bodies we are to find satisfaction, and that means strenuousness. Every power of mind and heart should go into the strenuousness of turning the natural into the spiritual by obeying the word of God regarding it. If we do not make the natural spiritual, it will become sordid; but when we become spiritual the natural is shot through with the glory of God.

Security of the Saint

"*Your wife shall be like a fruitful vine in the very heart of your house, your children like olive plants all around your table. Behold, thus shall the man be blessed who fears the* LORD" *(128:3-4).*

Today people are altogether ignoring the fact that God has anything to do with human relationships. If we get out of any setting of natural life which God has decreed we shall not be blessed. Take the commandment to "honor your father and mother," and apply it spiritually. I believe that many a life is hindered from entering into sanctification through not being properly related in disposition to father and mother. It is one of the most practical tests. Am I allowing inordinate affection in any relationship? or envy, or jealousy? If so I am certainly not finding blessing, it is getting dried up. I must maintain the spirit and disposition of my Lord and Master in all the ordinary relationships of life, then I shall realize the marvelous security of the saint.

Supremacy of Sincerity

"*The* LORD *shall bless you out of Zion, and may you see the good of Jerusalem all the days of your life*" *(128:5).*

Sincerity means "in the straight." Am I straight in my relationship to God and to other people? If I am, the Lord says He will bless me. "And may you see the good of Jerusalem all the days of your life." It is righteous behavior that brings blessing on others, and the heart of faith sees that God is working things out well.

Surroundings of Sanity

"Yes, may you see your children's children. Peace be upon Israel" (128:6).

It is in ordinary surroundings and among commonplace things that the blessing of God is to dwell and reveal itself. "Blessed are they that do His commandments, that they may have right to the tree of life, and may enter in through the gates into the city" (Revelation 22:14). Have I entered in through the gates? There is a time when the exceptional has to rule and the "right arm" has to go, but that is only a phase. Our Lord was brought up so much in ordinary surroundings that the religious people of His day said that He was "a gluttonous man, and a wine-bibber." His life was unassuming in its naturalness. Read the records of the forty days after the resurrection, they bear the mark of superb sanity. The test is not the success of a revival meeting, that may be questionable, but the success of living in the commonplace things that make life what it is, letting God carry out His purposes as He will.

THE HIGHEST GOOD

Summum Bonum

In speaking of the Highest Good as the theme of Ethics, Aristotle observes: "Every art and every kind of inquiry, and likewise every act and purpose, seems to aim at some good; and, since there are many kinds of actions, and many arts and sciences, it follows that there are many ends also. . . . And, if in what we do there be some end which we wish for on its own account, choosing all the others as a means to this, this will evidently be the best of all things. And surely from a practical point of view it much more concerns us to know this is good; for then, like archers shooting at a definite mark, we shall be more likely to attain what we want."—*The Ethic of Jesus,* Stalker.

All books on ethics talk about the *Summum Bonum,* that is, the greatest good is the highest end. In practical life we do not begin by thinking, we begin as common sense beings without thinking; we live first, and do things right and wrong and mixed up anyhow. The first practical thing we have to face in life is duty, and the Bible begins where common sense begins—in the practical domain. We have to get at what Jesus Christ taught was the highest good, then we can understand why He did not accept the standard of life that we accept, and why He plays havoc with all our lesser "goods" until we get to the supreme good He had in mind.

When we are born again we see things from a totally new perspective and we think we see all, then we go on a bit further, and when we get to the top of that peak there are regions beyond we never dreamed of, and so on. When we have got exhausted with the vistas before us we are prepared to hear Jesus say, "This is life eternal that they should know You the only true God" (John 17:3).

Evolution is simply a working way of explaining the growth and development of anything. When evolution is made a fetish and taken to mean God, then call it "bosh"; but evolution in a species, in an idea, in teaching, is exactly what our Lord taught: born of the Spirit and going on "till we all come . . . to the measure of the stature of the fullness of Christ." To understand means we can reconstruct a thing mentally and leave no element out. When we come to try and understand the highest good of our Lord, we must take it in His language, and it will take all time and eternity to understand what that Good is. Whether we live for the Highest Good does not depend on our understanding, but on whether we have the life of the Highest Good in us.

(1) *The Greatest Good is the Highest End*
(Matthew 7:4-14; 18:8-9; 19:16; 25:46).

"When Aristotle and the ancient thinkers spoke of the Highest Good, their meaning was, that in this earthly life of ours, there is for everyone a single supreme attainment, which if missed, will render life a failure, but, if gained, will render it a success" (Stalker).

The Shorter Catechism states, in answer to the question, "What is man's chief end?" that "Man's chief end is to glorify God and enjoy Him for ever." It is not what man puts in his body or on his body, but what he brings out of his body (see Matthew 15:17-20), and what he brings out of what he puts on his body—his money—that reveals what he considers his chief end. A great many people imagine they have glorified God when they have given two halfpennies for a penny, or have saved a halfpenny. The highest good to them is to keep economic relations right. The highest good from Jesus Christ's standpoint never dawns on them. The craze today is that the highest good is what a man has to live on: feed him, keep his body healthy, and his moral and religious life will be all right. That is the highest good according to the standard of many. As Christians it is more important to know how to live than what to live on. The attitude of the Christian is not, "I'm but a stranger here, heaven is my home," but rather "I'm *not* a stranger here." A stranger is exonerated from many things for which God holds us responsible. Jesus asked His Father to treat His disciples not as strangers but as inmates of the world and to keep them from the evil (John 17:13). We have to live in the heavenly places while here on earth.

(2) The Greatest Good is the Highest Evangel
(Matthew 4:23; 9:35; 11:5; 24:14; 26:13).

In the teaching of Jesus the term "the greatest good" is embodied in its most comprehensive sense in His use of the word "gospel." Our Lord in no way means what we commonly mean when we say "gospel," namely, salvation by faith in Jesus. The Bible never gives definitions, the Bible states facts, and the gospel that Jesus brought of good news about God is the most astounding thing the world ever heard, but it must be the gospel that Jesus brought. Whenever the gospel of Jesus loses the note of unutterable gladness, it is like salt that has lost its savor. We are apt to think of the gospel on the lines of spring cleaning. We have conceived of the kingdom of God in the time of the Millennium only, consequently when we come to the parables we are confused. The kingdom of God in this dispensation is the rule of God discerned by individuals alone (see

John 3:3). "Unless you are born from above," Jesus says, "you will never see the rule of God." It is not seen by the intellect. The rule of God which individual saints see and recognize is "without observation" in this dispensation. There is another dispensation coming when the whole world will see it as individuals have seen it.

"The kingdom of God is within you" (Luke 17:20-23). The blessedness of the gospel of the kingdom of God in this dispensation is that a man is born from above while he is below, and he actually sees with the eyes of his spirit the rule of God in the devil's territory. You will see how far we have got away from Jesus Christ's teaching. We bring in all kinds of things, we talk about salvation and sanctification and forgiveness of sins; Jesus did not mention these things to Nicodemus (He mentioned them later to the disciples). He said, "Be born from above and you will see the rule of God." It is an attitude of essential simplicity all through. Preaching what we call the gospel, that is, salvation from hell, does not appeal to men; but once get Jesus Christ to preach His own gospel and the Spirit of God to expound it, then men are hauled up at once.

Consideration of Several Beatitudes.

The drift of the Beatitudes has often been misunderstood. They have been supposed to describe the characteristics of true Christians, pronouncing those blessed who possess such-and-such qualities. But the structure is much more complex. . . . For example, one of the Beatitudes says, "Blessed are they who mourn": and, if we stop there, the statement is almost equivalent to the absurd saying, "Happy are the unhappy." The addition, however, of the words, "for they shall be comforted," makes all the difference. . . . And the same principle applies to all the Beatitudes. . . . Thus, mourning, hungering, persecution are not in themselves and by themselves, desirable, but the reverse; yet, taken along with what is given by Jesus to those thus circumstanced, they are blessedness itself (Stalker).

"*Blessed are the meek, for they shall inherit the earth.*" The gift here is the heritage of the earth by being fool enough to let other people have it at present. Jesus Christ taught that any one who possesses property of any nature has got to go through a baptism of bereavement in connection with it before he can be His disciple. The rich young ruler is a good specimen of possession (see Luke 18:22-3). The craze nowadays for those of us who have no property is to take the liberty of hauling to pieces those who have; but Jesus Christ turns it round the other way—"Do you possess anything, any property of pride, any sense of goodness, any virtue, any gift? Then you will have to go through intolerable bereavement before you can ever be My disciple." Intellectually that is inconceivable; spiritually it is clear to everyone who is rightly related to the Lord. This is where the obstinacy is revealed all through in us as disciples; we come up against this stone wall, and it produces obstinacy. The one great enemy of discipleship to Jesus Christ is spiritual obstinacy, the emphatic "I won't" which runs all through. Jesus says, "If you are to be My disciple this and that must go"; we are at liberty to say, "No, thank you," and to go away like the rich young ruler with fallen countenances and sorrowful because we have great possessions, we are somebodies, we have opinions of our own, we know exactly what we intend to do.

"*Blessed are the merciful, for they shall obtain mercy.*" As soon as we get right with God we are going to meet things that are contrary, we are going to meet un-merciful good people and un-merciful bad people, un-merciful institutions, un-merciful organizations, and we shall have to go through the discipline of being merciful to the merciless. It is much easier to say, "I won't bother my head with them"; then we shall never know the blessedness of obtaining God's mercy. Over and over again we will come up against things, and in order to get to the eternal blessedness Jesus Christ refers to we shall have to go through the unhappiness of doing something that the standards of men will be contemptuous over.

"*Blessed are the pure in heart, for they shall see God.*" How are we going to be pure in heart? We shall have to go through the humiliation of knowing we are impure. If you want to know what a pure heart is, read the life of the Lord Jesus Christ as recorded in the New Testament. His is a pure heart, anything less is not. Do you know the real panging misery of repentance? Think of the times (they are rare) when you have been in conscious touch with God—the moments when the simplicity of your heart-relationship to God, not your head, was undeterred by a sense of property or possession on your part—that was the time and place to see God.

(3) *The Greatest Good is the Healthiest Equity*
(Luke 6:20–23).

When we try to understand Jesus Christ's teaching with our heads we get into a fog. What Jesus Christ taught is only explainable to the personality of the mind in relation to the personality of Jesus Christ. It is a relationship of life, not of intellect. That is why Jesus said, "Unless you are converted and become as little children, you will by no means enter the kingdom of heaven." Our conception of things has to be torn to shreds until we realize that what makes a man a Christian is a simple heart-relationship to Jesus Christ, not intellectual conceptions.

This conception enlarges our horizon and enables us to understand why it took God's Son to preach the gospel, and why Jesus said, "The poor have the gospel preached to them" (Matthew 11:5). Why not the rich? The rich did not want it. "But even if our gospel is veiled," says Paul, "it is veiled"—from the publicans? No, "it is veiled to those who are perishing, whose minds the god of this age has blinded, who do not believe." That is the class for whom the gospel of Jesus has no meaning. A healthy-hided moral man does not want Jesus Christ; a ritualist does not want Jesus Christ, a rationalist does not want Jesus Christ. It is along this line we begin to understand why Jesus said, "I am not come to call the righteous," that is, the whole and the healthy, "but sinners to repentance." "I am come to those who mourn, to those who are afflicted, to those who are in a condition of insatiable thirst." Nothing will ever satisfy a man who is awakened but the supreme good—the gospel of God. The social worker who goes into work without this supreme good ends in heartbreak and disaster because all he succeeds in doing even while he satisfies lesser cravings is to render more intense the craving for something other—the one supreme God.

"Blessed are you when they revile and persecute you, and say all kinds of evil against you falsely for My sake. Rejoice and be exceeding glad." That is the mark of a Christian from our Lord's standpoint. Many of us are persecuted because we have crotchety notions of our own, but the mark of a disciple is suffering "for My sake." If we are foolish enough in the eyes of the world to order our life according to the rule of the kingdom of heaven, the only virtue will be, says Jesus, that men and women will hate you as they hated Me. Try to work your home life or your business life according to the rule of Jesus Christ and you will find that what He said is true, you will be put out of court as a fool, and we don't like to be thought fools. That is the persecution that many a man and woman has to go through if they are true to Jesus Christ, a continual semicultured sneering ridicule; nothing can stand that but absolute devotion to Jesus Christ, a creed will never stand it. Christianity is other-worldliness in the midst of this-worldliness. To apply the rule of the kingdom of God to our daily life is done not by our heads but by the obedience of our hearts. "If you are ever going to get the true blessedness," says Jesus, "it must be by living your life according to the rule of God." How are we going to discern the rule of God? Jesus told Nicodemus: "Unless one is born again, he cannot *see* the kingdom of God" and *enter into it* (John 3:3, 5). Then after we have entered into the kingdom of God, are we going to apply its rule to our bodily life, our mental life, our spiritual life? We are at liberty to stop short at any point, and our Lord will never cast it up at us; but think what we shall feel like when we see Him if all the "thank you" we gave Him for His unspeakable salvation was an obstinate determination to serve Him in our own way, not His.

Righteousness

Bear in mind that our human life viewed from a moral standpoint is a tragedy, and that preaching precepts while we ignore the cross of Jesus Christ is like giving "a pill to cure an earthquake," or a poultice for a cancer. Our attempts to face the problems of human life apart from Jesus Christ are futile. It is good for us to use our common sense and not live tragically, but remember, immediately you touch the moral problem you find that things are damnably wrong, the Book says so; they are so far wrong that it takes the cross of Jesus Christ to put them right, and we live in a fool's paradise if we ignore the terrific tragedy at the bottom of everything.

"Blessed are those who hunger and thirst for righteousness, for they shall be filled" (Matthew 5:6).

"Blessed are those who are persecuted for righteousness' sake, for theirs is the kingdom of heaven" (Matthew 5:10).

Most people use righteousness as a term for the behavior of man to man; and it includes this, but, when Christ speaks of hungering and thirsting after righteousness, and of being filled with it, there can be little doubt that, in accordance with the usage of His race, the prize He has in view is the favorable verdict of God on a man's character and conduct (Stalker).

The majority of us know nothing whatever about the righteousness that is gifted to us in Jesus Christ, we are still trying to bring human nature up to a pitch it cannot reach because there is something wrong with human nature. The old Puritanism which we are apt to ridicule did the same service for men that Pharisaism did for Saul, and that Roman Catholicism did for Luther; but nowadays we have no "iron" in us anywhere; we have no idea of righteousness, we do not care whether we are righteous or not. We have not only lost Jesus Christ's idea of righteousness, but we laugh at the Bible idea of righteousness; our god is the conventional righteousness of the society to which we belong.

The claim that our Lord was original is hopelessly wrong. He most emphatically took care not to be; He states that He came to fulfill what was already here but undiscerned. "Do not think that I came to destroy the Law or the Prophets. I did not come to destroy but to fulfill." That is why it is so absurd to put our Lord as a Teacher first, He is not first a Teacher, He is a Savior first. He did not come to give us a new code of morals: He came to enable us to keep a moral code we had not been able to fulfill. Jesus did not teach new things; he taught "as one having authority"— with power to make men into accordance with what He taught. Jesus Christ came *to make us holy,* not to tell us to be holy: He came to do for us what we could not do for ourselves.

The great tendency today is that we are looking for another teacher. The world is sick of teachers and of ideals; the point is, have we ever lived up to any of our ideals? It is not more ideals we want, but the power to live up to what we know we ought to and don't. It is shallowness, not ability, that makes people say we want more teaching and higher ideals—model Sunday School classes, model Bible classes; it is all model. "Do this and don't do that," but where is it being carried out? Jesus Christ does not add one burden to the lives of men; He imparts the power to live up to what we know we ought, that is the meaning of His salvation.

"For I say to you, that unless your righteousness exceeds the righteousness of the scribes and Pharisees, you will by no means enter the kingdom of heaven" (Matthew 5:20).

The sympathy of Christ with the training imparted by the Old Testament, and with the passion for righteousness thereby generated, is expressed very distinctly in the Sermon on the Mount, before the Preacher proceeds to the exposition of His own ideal; the motive underlying this declaration being a fear lest His subsequent references to the Old Testament should be understood as disparaging to its authority. In order to avoid this danger, He prefaced His exposition with the statement: "Think not that I am come to destroy the law or the prophets; I am not come to destroy, but to fulfill" (Stalker).

Jesus Christ contrasts His conception of righteousness with the one already familiar to His hearers. It is not a new gospel we need, that is the jargon of the hour; it is the old gospel put in terms that fit the present-day need, and for one man or one book that does that there are hundreds who tell us that what we want is a new gospel. What we want is men who have the grace of their Lord to face the present-day problems with the old gospel. What is the good of my talking to the crowd of today about the conceptions men had in Luther's day? The thing is, can I make the gospel I have meet the problems they are facing, and can I show them where other solutions are wrong? If not, I had better keep quiet. I have not been called of God to preach. The majority of us have our own idea of what the gospel is, but we live aloof from the time we belong to and what we preach is altogether apart from the lives of the folks we talk to.

Our Lord followed the simple line which the prophets took, He took the conceptions He knew men had and compared His own interpretations with theirs and made them judge, with what result? Absolute despair for everybody. Have we ever got hold of the idea that if Jesus Christ was only a teacher, He was the most tantalizing teacher that ever came to this earth? If Jesus Christ came to interpret to us a standard infinitely more profound than the one we already have, what is the good of it? He tells us that if we want to see God we must be pure in heart—how are we going to begin? He tells us to love our enemies, to bless them that curse us, to do good to them that hate us, to pray for those who despitefully use us, and persecute us—how can we begin to do it? If He is a Teacher only, then He is a most cruel Teacher, for He puts ideals before us that blanch us white to the lips and lead us to a hell of despair. But if He came to do something else as well as teach—if He came to remake us on the inside and put within us His own disposition of unsullied holiness, then we can understand why He taught like He did.

It is by facing our lives with the conceptions of Jesus that we understand the meaning of His cross. One of the most despairing things of our day is the shallow dogmatic competence of the people who tell us they believe in the teachings of Jesus but not in His atonement. The most unmitigated piece of nonsense human ears ever listened to! Believe in the teachings of Jesus—what is the good of it? What is the good of telling me that I have to be what I know I never can be if I live for a million years—perfect as God is perfect? What is the good of telling me I have to be a child of my Father in heaven and be like Him? We must rid our minds of the idea that is being introduced by the modern trend of things that Jesus Christ came to teach. The world is sick of teachers. Teachers never can do any good unless they can interpret the teaching that is already here.

"For I say to you, that unless your righteousness exceeds the righteousness of the scribes and Pharisees, you will by no means enter the kingdom of heaven" (Matthew 5:20).

"Having thus cleared the ground, the Great Teacher proceeds, in the Sermon on the Mount, to expound His conception of righteousness, and, in so doing, He adopts a method frequently resorted to by every expositor who knows his business: He contrasts the conception of the subject in His own mind with one already familiar to His hearers .... The righteousness of the scribes was external; that of Jesus is internal. Theirs was a righteousness in words and actions; His flows out from the innermost thoughts and feelings. Theirs was conventional—that is to say, it was intended for the eyes of society; His was a righteousness of the conscience having regard only to God" (Stalker).

"Unless your righteousness exceeds"—not be different from but "*excel*," that is, we have to be all they are and infinitely more! We have to be right in our external behavior, but we have to be as right, and "righter," in our internal behavior. We have to be right in our words and actions, but we have to be as right in our thoughts and feelings. We have to be right according to the conventions of the society of godly people, but we have also to be right in conscience towards God. Nominal Christians are often without the ordinary moral integrity of the man who does not care a bit about Jesus Christ; not because they are hypocrites, but because we have been taught for generations to think on one aspect only of Jesus Christ's salvation—the revelation that salvation is not merited by us, but is the sheer sovereign act of God's grace in Christ Jesus. A grand marvelous revelation fact, but Jesus says we have got to say "Thank you" for our salvation, and the "Thank you" is that our righteousness is to exceed the righteousness of the most moral man on earth.

Jesus not only demands that our external life is above censure but that we are above censure where God sees us. We see the meaning now of saying that Jesus is the most tantalizing Teacher: He demands that we be so pure that God who sees to the inmost springs of our motives, the inmost dreams of our dreams, sees nothing to censure. We may go on evolving and evolving, but we shall never produce that kind of purity. Then what is the good of teaching it? Listen: "If we walk in the light as He is in the light, we have fellowship with one another, *and the blood of Jesus Christ His Son cleanses us from all sin.*" That is the gospel; Jesus Christ claims that He can take a man or woman who is fouled in the springs of their nature by heredity and make them as pure as He is Himself. That is why He teaches what He does, and it is His standard we are to be judged by if we are His disciples. No wonder the disciples when they heard Jesus speak, said, "Who then can be saved?" The greatest philosophy ever produced does not come within a thousand leagues of the fathomless profundity of our Lord's statements, for example, "Learn from Me, for I am gentle and lowly in heart" (Matthew 11:29). If Jesus Christ cannot produce a gentleness and lowliness of heart like His own, Christianity is nonsense from beginning to end, and His teaching had better be blotted out.

The crucial point of the whole matter is our personal relationship to Jesus Christ. It is far more honest to discard Him absolutely than to play the fool with your own soul and pretend you agree with His teaching while you despise the very central part of it. No wonder Jesus said to a fine godly old man, "Do not marvel that I said to you, 'You must be born again.' " If we cannot be made all over again on the inside and indwelt by the Spirit of God, and made according to the teaching of the Sermon on the Mount, then fling your New Testament away, for it will put before you an ideal you cannot reach.

The only way to get out of our smiling complacency about salvation and sanctification is to look at Jesus Christ for two minutes and then read Matthew 5:43-48 and see who He tells us we are to be like, God Almighty, and every piece of smiling spiritual conceit will be knocked out of us for ever, and the one dominant note of the life will be Jesus Christ first, Jesus Christ second, and Jesus Christ third, and our own whiteness nowhere. Never look to your own whiteness; look to Jesus and get power to live as He wants; look away for one second and all goes wrong.

"When the Son of man comes, will He really find faith on the earth?" We all have faith in good principles, in good management, in good common sense, but who among us has faith in Jesus Christ? Physical courage is grand, moral courage is grander, but the man who trusts Jesus Christ in the face of the terrific problems of life is worth a whole crowd of heroes.

Missing It

Anything Jesus Christ revealed may be missed. The disbelief of the human mind always wastes itself in the sentimental idea that God would never let us miss the greatest good. Jesus says He will, that is why we don't like Him, and that is why the teaching of today is not the teaching of the Jesus Christ of the New Testament.

(1) What if a Man Gain the Whole World?
(Mark 8:34-35).

(a) His Point of View
"Whoever desires to come after Me, let him deny himself, and take up his cross, and follow Me. For whoever desires to save his life will lose it, but whoever loses his life for My sake and the gospel's will save it."

"However the end of life may be conceived—whether as Blessedness, or as the kingdom of God, or as Righteousness—one thing is indubitable in the entire teaching of Jesus—that He looks upon the end of life as capable of being missed" (Stalker).

The word translated "soul" or "life" may be equally well translated "himself," and the verses mean just what they say. Jesus is not defining the great fundamental doctrine of personality, He is talking about the man himself, and the person who lives, and with whom we come in contact. Jesus says if a man gains himself, he loses himself and if he loses himself for His sake, he gains himself.

Beware of introducing the idea of time; the instant the Spirit of God touches your spirit, it is manifested in the body. Do not get the idea of a three-storied building with a vague, mysterious, ethereal upper story called spirit, a middle story called soul, and a lower story called body. We are personality, which shows itself in three phases—spirit, soul, and body. Never think that what energizes the spirit takes time before it gets into the soul and body, it shows itself instantly, from the crown of the head to the soles of the feet.

Jesus says that men are capable of missing the supreme good and His point of view is not acceptable to us because we do not believe we are capable of missing it. We are far removed from Jesus Christ's point of view today, we take the natural rationalistic line, and His teaching is no good whatever unless we believe the main gist of His gospel: that we have to have something planted into us by supernatural grace. Jesus Christ's point of view is that a man may miss the chief good; we like to believe we will end all right somehow, but Jesus says we won't. If my feet are going in one direction, I cannot advance one step in the opposite direction unless I turn right around.

(b) Preaching from that Point of View

"When He speaks of Blessedness, He at the same time utters woes which will be the portion of some instead of blessedness; when He speaks of the Kingdom, He distinctly thinks of some that will not be able to enter into it; and when He speaks of righteousness, He glances at many who are living in unrighteousness. In short, there is a considerable portion of the words of Christ occupied with the description and denunciation of sin" (Stalker).

We have, as Christian disciples, to recognize continually that much of what is called Christianity today is not the

Christianity of the New Testament; it is distinctly different in generation and manifestation. Jesus is not the fountainhead of modern Christianity; He is scarcely thought about. Christian preachers, Sunday school teachers, religious books, all without any apology patronize Jesus Christ and put Him on one side. We have to learn that to stand true to Jesus Christ's point of view means the ostracism that was brought on Him; most of us know nothing whatever about it. The modern view looks upon human nature as pathetic: men and women are poor ignorant babes in the wood who have lost themselves. Jesus Christ's view is totally different, He does not look on men and women as babes in the wood, but as sinners who need saving, and the modern mind detests His view. Our Lord's teaching is based on something we violently hate—His doctrine of sin; we do not believe it unless we have had a radical dealing with God on the line of His teaching.

Remember that a disciple is committed to much more than belief in Jesus; he is committed to his Lord's view of the world, of men, of God, and of sin. Take stock of your views and compare them with the New Testament, and never get tricked into thinking that the Bible does not mean what it says when it disagrees with you. Disagree with what our Lord says by all means if you like, but never say that the Bible does not mean what it says.

(c) His Procedure and Others'

"This is the point at which the ethical teaching of Jesus differs most widely from the similar teaching of philosophy. The ethics of the philosophers bear a considerable resemblance to the teaching of Jesus in so far as the setting up of an ideal of character and conduct is concerned; but little or nothing is said by philosophers about the inability of men to attain to the standard, or of the manifold forms of failure exhibited in actual experience" (Stalker).

People say, "Oh yes, the Sermon on the Mount is very beautiful, our ideals must be better than we can attain, we shall drift into the Lord's ideals in time somehow or other"; but Jesus says we won't, we will miss them. "The manifold forms of failure exhibited in actual experience" is ignored by other ethical teachers. They say it is never too late to mend—it is; that you can start again—you cannot; that you can make the past as though it had never been—it is impossible; that anyway you can put yourself in such a condition that what you have done need not count—you cannot, and our Lord is the only One who recognizes these things. We think because we fail and forget it, therefore it is overlooked by God—it is not. Jesus Christ's standard remains, and the entrance into His kingdom and into a totally new life is by regeneration, and in no other way. The teachings and standards of Jesus, which are so distasteful to modern Christianity, are based on what our Lord said to Nicodemus: "Do not marvel that I said to you, 'You must be born again' "; otherwise our Lord was a dreamer. The reason we do not see the need to be born from above is that we have a vast capacity for ignoring facts. People talk about the evolution of the race. The writers of today seem to be incapable of a profound understanding of history, they write glibly about the way the race is developing, where are their eyes and their reading of human life as it is? We are not evolving and developing in any sense to justify what is known as evolution. We have developed in certain domains but not in all. We are nowhere near the massive, profound intellectual grasp of the men who lived before Christ was born. What brain today can come near Plato or Socrates? And yet people say we are developing and getting better, and we are laying the flattering unction to our souls that we have left Jesus Christ and His ideas twenty centuries behind. No wonder Jesus said that if we stand by Him and take His point of view, men will hate us as they hated Him.

"In spite of his tendency to self-satisfaction, every man is aware some time or other of his own broken bones, and he knows that there must be death before there is any prospect of climbing the heights of moral attainment" (Stalker).

Have you ever noticed that in some moods you have battled bitterly against the position you know to be right, and all your tirade against it is born of a fear lest after all it might be wrong? That is the real attitude of men and women, they will accept any amount of subterfuges, but right down underneath they have a superb contempt for anything less than that which goes to the root of the matter, and the only One who does is the Lord Jesus Christ. Sooner or later every human heart flings away as chaff the idea that we are developing and growing better.

(2) *What if a Man Lose Himself?*
(a) The Possibility of the Question
"For what will it profit a man if he gains the whole world, and lose his own soul? Or what will a man give in exchange for his soul?" (Mark 8:36-37).

"Jesus habitually saw with the mind's eye the spiritual development which those around Him might have attained had their desires been fixed more steadily on the true end of life" (Stalker).

"The idea seems to be, that, even though it does not come to absolute loss, yet if gaining the world involve damage to the self, the moral personality—taint, lowering of the tone, vulgarizing of the soul—we lose much more than we gain" (Bruce).

In the training of art students, the master does not merely tell them what is wrong in a design, he puts the right design beside the wrong and lets them judge for themselves, and that is exactly what Jesus Christ did all through the Sermon on the Mount.

Do I accept the possibility that I may miss the highest good? There is a sentimental notion that makes us make ourselves out worse than we think we are, because we have a lurking suspicion that if we make ourselves out amazingly bad, someone will say, "Oh no, you are not as bad as that"; but Jesus says we are worse. Our Lord never trusted any one, "for He knew what was in man"; but He was not a cynic for He had the profoundest confidence in what He could do for every individual, consequently He was never in a moral or intellectual panic, as we are, because we will put our confidence in people and in the things that Jesus put no confidence in. Paul says, "Don't glory in men; don't say, I am of Paul, or I am of Apollos, and don't think of yourself more highly than you ought to think, but think according to the measure of faith, that is, according to what the grace of God has done in you." Never trust (in the fundamental meaning of the word) any other saving Jesus Christ. That will mean you will never be unkind to anybody on the face of the earth, whether it be a degraded criminal or an upright moral person, because you have learned that the only thing to depend on in people is what God has done in them. When you come to work for Jesus Christ, always ask yourself, "Do I believe Jesus Christ can do anything for that case?" Am I as confident in His power as He is in His own? If you deal with people without any faith in Jesus Christ it will crush the very life out of you. If we believe in Jesus Christ, we can face every problem the world holds.

(b) Property and Perdition

"Take heed and beware of covetousness, for one's life does not consist in the abundance of the things he possesses" (Luke 12:15).

"What He thought of most frequently as impeding the growth of true manhood was the pursuit of wealth and property" (Stalker).

How many people do you know who have their godliness incarnated in economy? Are you one of them? If we can save and do justly with money, we are absolutely certain we are right in the sight of God. The thing about our Lord and His teaching that puts Him immeasurably away from us nowadays is that He is opposed to all possessions, not only of money and property, but any kind of possession. That is the thing that makes Him such a deep-rooted enemy to the modern attitude to things. The two things around which our Lord centered His most scathing teaching were money and marriage, because they are the two things that make men and women devils or saints. Covetousness is the root of all evil, whether it shows itself in money matters or in any way.

(c) Poverty and Perdition

"But seek first the kingdom of God and His righteousness, and all these things shall be added to you" (Matthew 6:33).

"But Jesus was hardly less sensible of the danger to which the poor were exposed of missing the prize through an opposite cause—on account, not of the glamour of riches, but the pressure of poverty.... His was not a gospel of meat and drink, of loaves and fishes, of better clothes and better houses" (Stalker).

Jesus Christ nowhere stands with the antiproperty league. It is an easy business for me to mentally satirize the man who owns land and money when I don't. It is easy for me to talk about what I could do with a thousand dollars if I had it; the test is what I do with the two dollars I have got. It may be hard for a rich man to enter into the kingdom of heaven, but it is just as hard for a poor man to seek first the kingdom of God. It is not eternal perdition, it is the perdition of losing the soul for this life. Jesus thought as much of the possibility of losing the highest good through poverty as through riches. His own followers were poor, yet He said to them, "seek first—bread and cheese? money? a new situation? clothing? food?" No, "the kingdom of God and His righteousness, and all these thing shall be added to you." Did He know what He was talking about, this poor carpenter who had not a pillow of His own and never enough money to pay a night's lodging and yet spoke like that, and who also said that "the cares of this world and the deceitfulness of riches choke the word, and it becomes unfruitful?

Have I ever tried to practice one thing that Jesus taught in the Sermon on the Mount? Tolstoy blundered in applying the Sermon on the Mount practically without insisting on the need to be born again of the Spirit of God first; but I am taking for granted that we are born again, now try putting into practice something Jesus said, and if what He said does not prove true, say so, but try it. For instance, "Give to him who asks you." "Yes," you say, "and be surrounded at once with a crowd of beggars!" Is the Almighty absolutely powerless? We argue like pagans and jargonize like saints. The sentimental jargon in our prayer meetings is exactly like the New Testament language, while in practice we are pagans as if Jesus had never said a word. What man who has never allowed God to lift him up would dare to stand before his fellow creatures and lift up the standard of God? There would be deep condemnation in every message he gave.

Our Lord based a man's self-realization on his spiritual relationship to God. Carlyle estimated human beings by their brains and came to the conclusion that half the human race were fools. Imagine measuring a man by the amount of gray matter in his cranium! You cannot judge a man by his head, but only by his character. One of the greatest disasters in human life is our wrong standards of judgment, we will judge men by their brains. Jesus never did. Jesus judged men and women by their relationship to His Father, an implicit relationship. The brain is nothing more than a marvelous machine for expressing a man's conception of things, and when our hearts and lives are right with God, our brains are a means of expressing a particular conception which comes from our Lord. Never partake of the cynical view of life. Jesus Christ estimates that a man's real soul life is his relationship to God and nothing else, and Paul said, "Let no one by his philosophy beguile you away from this simplicity"—the simplicity of the life "hidden with Christ in God."

Irresponsibility

Every Christian worker has to decide this question: Is Jesus Christ's mind infallible, or is the modern Western mind infallible? The tendency abroad today is to think ourselves infallible, and the Bible a jumble of the most extraordinary stuff, good stuff, but we cannot be expected to accept all its views. That means we believe ourselves more likely to be infallible than Jesus Christ. We would repudiate this statement if made baldly, but we all act as if it were true, we all take for granted that Jesus Christ's teachings are nonsense; we treat them with respect and reverence, but we do not do anything else with them, we do not carry them out.

For the past three hundred years men have been pointing out how similar Jesus Christ's teachings are to other good teachings. We have to remember that Christianity, if it is not a supernatural miracle, is a sham.

(1) This Life's Use Wasted

"For what will it profit a man if he gains the whole world, and loses his own soul?" (Mark 8:36).

"The most literal meaning of losing one's life is, of course, dying by accident; . . . if a man loses his life by accident what is the whole world to him?" (Stalker)

Jesus says that life is the opportunity God gives to man to do his life work; that means that God has no respect whatever for our programs and machinery. Our Lord insists on one thing only, God's purpose for him; He pays not the remotest attention to civilized forces, He estimates nothing but one standard. According to our standards He was idle; for three years He walked about saying things. It is only by putting these violent contrasts before our minds that we understand how different our Lord's standpoint to life is compared with ours. We bend the whole energy of our lives to machinery, and when an accident happens and the machinery breaks up we say, "What a disaster." Probably it was the emancipation of the man's life. We make nests here and there, competences here and there, but God has no respect for any of them; at any minute He may send a wind and over goes the whole thing. The one thing God is after is character.

"Not only has the Creator appointed to every human being, in the constitution of his manhood, a certain stature to which he may and ought to attain; but He has appointed a corresponding task for him to fulfill, determined by the providential circumstances in which he is placed. In fact, this is his life; and not to fulfill this God-appointed purpose of his existence is to lose his life" (Stalker).

It is along these fundamental lines that we understand why the Bible says, "There is a way that seems right to a man, but its end is the way of death"; why Solomon said, "God made man upright, but they have sought out many schemes"; and why he further said, "Trust in the LORD with all your heart, and lean not on your own understanding"; and why our Lord said, "Do not let your heart be troubled." The characteristic of a man who is not based on the issue of his life is an incessant cunning, crafty, commercial worry. Our Lord was absolutely devoid of that. What we call responsibility our Lord never had, and what He called responsibility people are without. People do not care a bit for Jesus Christ's notion of their lives, and Jesus does not care for our notions. There is the antagonism. If we were to estimate ourselves from our Lord's standpoint, very few of us would be considered disciples.

"*This idea lay near to the heart of Jesus, first of all, in relation to Himself. He thoroughly realized, from first to last, that He had a work to do, so accurately arranged and fitted to the length of His life that every hour had its own part of the whole to clear off, and He was not allowed either to anticipate or lag behind*" (Stalker).

Today we hold conferences and conventions and give reports and make our programs. None of these things were in the life of Jesus, and yet every minute of His life He realized that He was fulfilling the purpose of His Father (John 9:4). How did He do it? By maintaining the one relationship, and it is that one relationship He insists on in His disciples, and it is the one we have lost in the rubbish of modern civilization. If we try to live the life Jesus Christ lived, modern civilization will fling us out like waste material; we are no good, we do not add anything to the hard cash of the times we live in, and the sooner we are flung out the better.

In John's gospel this aspect of our Lord's life is more elaborately worked out than anywhere else. It is indicated in other gospels (see Luke 2:49; 8:32; 12:50). Jesus knew He was here for His Father's purpose and He never allowed the cares of civilization to bother Him. He did nothing to add to the wealth of the civilization in which He lived, He earned nothing. Modern civilization would not have tolerated Him for two minutes.

"*It will be remembered how frequently He represented this life as a trust or stewardship*" (See Luke 19:13). "*On one occasion Jesus manifested extraordinary irritation . . . at the sight of a tree that was barren (Mark 11:12-14); but this was a manifestation of an impatience, which beset Him always, with objects that were not answering the end of their existence*" (Stalker).

In our Lord's mind any created thing which fails in making anything of its purpose is contemptible (see Luke 13:6-9). Jesus' attitude to Roman and Grecian civilization was one of superb contempt. Our attitude to Greece and Rome is one of unrestrained reverence, with not so much as the cast of an eye for Jesus Christ. Our Lord followed life from His Father's standpoint, today we are caught up in the show of things. Take the Bible attitude to men on the whole, civilizations are dispatched at a minute's notice, armies come together and annihilate one another and God seems to pay no attention. His attitude is one which makes us blaspheme and say that He does not care an atom for human beings. Jesus Christ says He does, He says He is a Father, and that He, Jesus, is exactly like His Father. The point is that Jesus saw life from God's standpoint, and we don't. We won't accept the responsibility of life as God gives it to us, we only accept responsibility as we wish to take it, and the responsibility we wish to take is to save our own skins, make comfortable positions for ourselves and those we are related to, exert ourselves a little to keep ourselves clean and vigorous and upright; but when it comes to following out what Jesus says, His sayings are nothing but jargon. We name the name of Christ but we are not based on His one issue of life, and Jesus says, "What will it profit a man if he gains the whole world"—and he can easily do it—"and lose his own soul?"

(2) *This Soul's Way Missed*

"Or what will a man give in exchange for his soul?" (Mark 8:37).

The attitude of our Lord's mind is this, that the eternal

condition of a man's spirit is determined by his soul life in this order of things.

The loss of oneself in missing one's opportunities of moral and spiritual development . . . . may end in the loss of the 'soul' in the awful sense of being cast away for ever. On this solemn subject the teaching of our Lord is extraordinarily copious; indeed, it is to Him that the popular conceptions about a Day of Judgment and the retributions of a future existence are due" (Stalker).

The modern Christian laughs at the idea of a final judgment. That shows how far we can stray away if we imbibe the idea that the modern mind is infallible and not our Lord. To His mind at least the finality of moral decision is reached in this life. There is no aspect of our Lord's mind that the modern mind detests so fundamentally as this one. It does not suit us in any shape or form. The average modern mind reads such passages as Luke 16:23-24 and says our Lord was only using figurative language.

If the picture is so dreadful figuratively, what must the reality be like? The things our Lord talks about are either arrant nonsense or they are a revelation of things that the common sense of man can never guess. The attitude of Jesus is outside our standards in every way. We must face the music today as we have never faced it. Christianity is a complete sham or a supernatural miracle from beginning to end; immediately we admit it is a miracle we are responsible for walking in the light of what we know Jesus Christ to be.

To our Lord's mind the definiteness of the finality of punishment was as clear as could be, and nothing but lack of intelligence ever makes us say He did not put it in that way, and if those of us who take Him to be Lord and Master, take Him to mean what He says, where ought we to be in regard to these questions? The majority of us are apologetic about the teachings of Jesus, we are much too easily cowed by modern good taste. The modern mind is the infallible god to the majority of us. A man like Blatchford, who simply puts Jesus Christ on one side is in a much more wholesome state. It is far better to do that than accept Jesus and leave out what we don't like. That is to be a traitor and a deserter.

The parables in Matthew 25 are three aspects of the divine estimate of life. Beware of being an ingenious interpreter. You will always find at the basis of our Lord's parables and illustrations a fundamental consistency to His revelation.

The parable of the ten virgins reveals that it is fatal from our Lord's standpoint to live this life without preparation for the life to come. That is not the exegesis, it is the obvious underlying principle.

The parable of the talents is our Lord's statement with regard to the danger of leaving undone the work of a lifetime.

And the description of the last judgment is the picture of genuine astonishment on the part of both the losers and the gainers of what they had never once thought about.

To be accustomed to our Lord's teaching is not to ask, "What must I do to be good?" but, "What must I do to be saved?" How long does it take us to know what the true meaning of our life is? One half second?

> Oh, we're sunk enough here, God knows!
>   But not quite so sunk that moments,
> Sure tho' seldom, are denied us,
>   When the spirit's true endowments
> Stand out plainly from its false ones,
>   And apprise it if pursuing
> Or the right way or the wrong way,
>   To its triumph or undoing.

> There are flashes struck from midnights
>   There are fire-flames noondays kindle,
> Whereby piled-up honors perish,
>   Whereby swollen ambitions dwindle,
> While just this or that poor impulse,
>   Which for once had play unstifled,
> Seems the sole work of a lifetime
>   That away the rest have trifled.

There never was anyone who did not have one moment when all the machinery tumbled away and he saw the meaning of his life. God pays not the remotest attention to our civilized cultures and our attitude to things, because that is not what we are here for. We are here for one thing—to glorify God. That is where we join issue with the Lord Jesus Christ today, and we look at every other thing as life— "What shall we eat? What shall we drink? What shall we wear?" Our Lord came for one purpose only, to reveal God, and to get men to be spiritually real.

If we would have the blunt courage of ordinary human beings and face the teachings of Jesus, we would have to come to one of two conclusions—either the conclusion His contemporaries came to, that He was demon-possessed, or else to the conclusion the disciples came to, that He is God Incarnate. Jesus Christ will not water down His teaching to suit our weakness in any shape or form; He will not allow us to cringe in the tiniest degree. Whenever there is a trace of cringing or whining, or wanting something different from what He wants, it is the stern front of the Son of God uncloaking sin every time we look at Him; but if we come as paupers, what happens? Exactly the opposite. He will lift us up and wash us whiter than snow, and put the Holy Spirit in us and place us before the throne of God, undeserving of censure, by the sheer omnipotence of His atonement.

What we have to get hold of in our moral lives is that Jesus Christ demands that we live His holy life out naturally. Despair is always the gateway of faith. "If you can believe, all things are possible to him who believes." So many of of us get depressed about ourselves, but when we get to the point where we are not only sick of ourselves, but sick to death, then we shall understand what the atonement of the Lord Jesus Christ means. It will mean that we come to Him without the slightest pretence, without any hypocrisy, and say, "Lord, if You can make anything of me, do it," and He will do it. The Lord can never make a saint out of a good man, He can only make a saint out of three classes of people—the godless one, the weak one, and the sinful one, and no one else, and the marvel of the gospel of God's grace is that Jesus Christ can make us naturally what He wants us to be.

The Base Impulse

But, ah, through all men some base impulse runs,
The brute the father, and the men the sons,
Which if one harshly sets himself to subdue,
With fiercer indolence it boils anew,
He ends the worst who with best hopes began,
How hard is this, how like the lot of man!

Experimentally the meaning of life is to attain the excellency of a broken heart, for that alone entails repentance and acceptance, the two great poles of Bible revelation. "The sacrifices of God are a broken spirit"—why, we do not know, but God has made it so. The one thing we are after is to avoid getting broken hearted.

The base impulse revealed itself in the time of our Lord in three great types of sin—the sin of the publicans, the sin of the Pharisees, and the sin of the Sadducees.

"In every country there is a lost class, a class that has given way to the sins of the flesh till its sin can no longer be concealed. What others do by stealth, they do openly. Such a class existed in our Lord's day in Palestine, and the popular names for them in that day were publicans and sinners, or publicans and harlots, or the lost sheep of the house of Israel . . . . The attitude of Jesus to this class was one of the most singular and characteristic features of His career, and, when fully understood, reveals more clearly perhaps than any other circumstance the secret of His mission" (Stalker).

It is remarkable how little Jesus directed His speech

against carnal and public sins, though He showed plenty of prophetic indignation against the sins of a wholly different class. He preached His grandest sermon to a bad, ignorant woman (John 4:10-14), and one of His most prominent disciples was a publican named Matthew. The one man He ever said He wanted to stay with was another publican called Zaccheus, and some of the most fathomless things He said were in connection with a notoriously bad woman (Luke 7:36-50). It is along this line that we can understand why the Pharisees were sick to the heart and disgusted with Jesus Christ, why they called Him "a friend of the publicans and sinners!" We would have done exactly the same today in spite of all our religious sentiments. We gloss over our Lord's actions with our civilized conceptions and destroy the meaning of His gospel.

Our Lord's conduct was not due to any insensibility to the wickedness of open and carnal sins, nor that He was lenient to those sins: He drew near to those sins to make them for ever impossible in the lives of those guilty of them. Jesus roused the conscience of the very worst of them by presenting the highest good. We are apt to forget that our Lord's parables in Luke 15 say just what they do. Never take the fifteenth chapter of Luke as an exposition of the gospel first; it is our Lord's apologia; He is explaining to the Pharisees why He is here.

(1) *The Pharisaic Invincibility*

In interpreting our Lord's teaching, watch carefully who He is talking to; the parable of the prodigal son was a stinging lash to the Pharisees. We need to be reminded of the presentation of Jesus in the New Testament for the Being pictured to us nowadays would not perturb anybody; but He aroused His whole nation to rage. Read the records of

His ministry and see how much blazing indignation there is in it. For thirty years Jesus did nothing, then for three years He stormed every time He went down to Jerusalem. Josephus says He tore through the temple courts like a madman. We hear nothing about that Jesus Christ today. The meek and mild Being pictured today makes us lose altogether the meaning of the cross. We have to find out why Jesus was beside Himself with rage and indignation at the Pharisees and not with those given over to carnal sins. Which state of society is going to stand a ripping and tearing Being like Jesus Christ who drags to the ground the highest respected pillars of its civilized society, and shows that their respectability and religiosity is built on a much more abominable pride than the harlot's or the publican's? The latter are disgusting and coarse, but these men have the very pride of the devil in their hearts.

Ask yourself, then, what is it that awakens indignation in your heart? Is it the same kind of thing that awakened indignation in Jesus Christ? The thing that wakens indignation in us is the thing that upsets our present state of comfort and society. The thing that made Jesus Christ blaze was pride that defied God and prevented Him from having His right with human hearts. Sin is the independence of human nature which God created turning against God. Holiness is this same independence turning against sin. Sin is not doing wrong things, it is wrong being. Sins are wrong acts; sin is an independence that will not bow its neck to God, that defies God and all He represents, that will not go to the excellency of a broken heart. It is that class who stand for independence in art and culture; it is not for them a question of right or wrong, but of pleasing the senses. The greatest pillars of art and culture are erected on these lines and Jesus Christ pulls down the whole temple, because we cannot build temples of art on this earth at all; they will be built in heaven when the foundations are pure. The refinements of art and culture are all in opposition to the tumbling in crisis of God in the Incarnation.

(2) *The Pride of Integrity*

The conspicuous point of view in which the Pharisees always figure in the gospels is as incapable of repentance. Self-knowledge is the first condition of repentance. Watch Jesus Christ whenever there is the tiniest sign of repentance, He is the incarnation of forgiving and forgetting, and He says that is God's nature. "I am not come to call the righteous, but sinners to repentance." Remember, that kind of statement hits the Pharisees to the very core of their being. Could they listen patiently to a Man like that? Jesus was killed for His words, He would not have been crucified if He had kept quiet. It was the ruthless way He went straight to the very root of Pharisaism that enraged them until they became the devil incarnate and crucified the Son of God. *Calvary* means "the place of a skull," and that is where our Lord is always crucified, in the culture and intellect of men who will not have self-knowledge given by the light of Jesus Christ.

(3) *Sensible Rationalism*

The Sadducee is the type of person who in all ages destroys the treasure of the spirit; he is a common-sense individual.

"There are some people to whom it is never safe to show any valued possession. . . . Now and then someone with the bump of destruction will push his way into our holy of holies, and deface what he considers our idols and leave us sad. . . . Unfold a scheme, a dream, a theory, a long-cherished recollec-

tion within the reach of a man who loves destruction, and he will reduce it to nothing. Even a book, that treasure which stands half-way between the tangible and the intangible, is not safe with him, he will turn its pages into ridicule, and give it back with half its charm destroyed" (Stalker).

Thomas Carlyle utterly destroyed the early faith of his wife and never gave her anything in its stead, and Mrs. Carlyle's letters, gifted with the most amazing literary ability and mentality, are wilted and sad, like her face, because he destroyed in the true spirit of the Sadducee her holy of holies and gave her nothing in its place. This line of thought makes us understand our Lord's attitude to the Sadducees, and why He said, "Don't cast your pearls before swine." There are some things we must never show to anyone. Like children, we all think that we ought to show our cherished possessions, we ought not; there are Sadducees everywhere. You rarely find them people of uncouth speech, but rather the opposite.

We have all met people who act like an east wind, our mental horizon gets lower and we feel unmitigatedly mean and despicable. When Jesus Christ came near people, He convicted them of sin, but He convicted them also of this, that they could be like He was if they would only come to Him.

"*The Sadducees were the anti-Pharisaic party, and they went as far in believing too little as the Pharisees in the direction of believing too much. They were the skeptical religious party. Their beliefs lacked warmth and conviction. The weakness of the religious sentiment in them was partly the cause and partly the effect of another characteristic, viz. worldliness. The spiritual and eternal stirred them but faintly, consequently they had a more tenacious hold on the concerns of this present life*" (Stalker).

Watch the difference between the faces marred by sin and those marred by coming in contact with the Sadducees, who have all their inner shrines destroyed and nothing given in their place; the latter have a look of withered, mean sanity. Sin does not produce it, it is the effect of the presence of this monster—the rational, healthy-minded Sadducee; this "monster" has been inside the Christian Church for the past twenty centuries, and is one of the problems that has to be faced. There are comparatively few Pharisees today, the greater number are Sadducees, who back up their little bits of common sense against all that Jesus Christ said and against everything anyone says who has had a vision of things differing from common sense.

(4) *Sensible Ruling*

"The Sadducees were the ruling class and the priestly party from the date of the Babylonian exile. Such priests have continually emerged in the affairs of God, and they are much more interested in the affairs of the visible world and but faintly tinged with the hope or spirit of the world invisible" (Stalker).

This is the type that perfectly exhibits the Sadducee of our Lord's day. It is not the brutal skeptic who is the Sadducee, he does not destroy anybody's shrines, it is the religious man or woman with particularly bright conceptions of their own, but who are far more concerned with the visible success of this world than with anything else. You go to them with some insurgent doubt in your mind, and they smile at you and say, "Oh don't exercise your mind on those things, it is absurd." That is the Sadducee who has done more to deface in modern life what Jesus Christ began to do than all the blackguardism and drunkenness in our modern civilization. The subtle destruction of all that stands for the invisible is what is represented by the Sadducee.

It is necessary to get the historical atmosphere and setting of our Lord's life in order to understand the historical exegesis of His teaching. Most of us only know the spiritual exegesis, we come with our spiritual illumination and take incidents out of the Bible—"I don't care about their historic exegesis, I simply take them as expressing my own spiritual condition." That is not the thing for a student to do; a student has to divide rightly the word of truth, and to find out the historic background of Jesus Christ's teaching.

In Luke 16:19-31 we get a good picture of our Lord's attitude to the Sadducees. The rich man *"lived to dine and to wear sumptuous clothing, neither bestowing on the poor any generosity commensurate with his means nor remembering that he was an heir of eternity, and herein is the great moral principle, viz. that of not doing being as guilty as doing, and that the Judge will accept no excuse for a life not marked by unselfishness up to the means of its opportunity" (Stalker).*

If we know that we have received the unmerited favor of God and we do not give unmerited favor to other people, we are damned in that degree. The best and most spiritual people today turn Jesus Christ's teaching out of court. They say He could never have meant what He said, and, we have to use common sense. If we apply common sense we run the risk of being Sadducees. What common sense person would carry out the Sermon on the Mount? It is the Sadducee who withers up the true spirit of devotion to God in our life by a "squirt" of common sense, because the common sense comes from a background of infidelity against God's rule. We are measured by what we do according to what we have. Some people only give to the undeserving, because they imagine they deserve all they have. Our Lord

The Base Impulse

says, Give, not because they deserve it, but because I tell you to.

"*Jesus reveals in the parable of the rich man (Luke 12:16-21) that his mind and heart have been entirely absorbed with property. About his soul and eternity he has manifested no concern, he heaped up treasure but was not rich towards God*" (Stalker).

Treasure in heaven is the wealth of character that has been earned by standing true to the faith of Jesus, not to the faith in Jesus. Our Lord's advice to the rich young ruler was, "Sell all that you have and give to the poor, and come, follow Me, and you will have treasure in heaven." That is, have faith for the things Jesus Christ stood for, and anybody who is fool enough to conduct his life with Jesus Christ as absolute Master will realize what Jesus said, "Men shall separate you from their company . . . and cast out your name as evil." Many of us are saved by the skin of our teeth, we are comfortably settled for heaven, that is all we care for, now we can make a pile on earth. There are plenty of people who give their testimony all right in meetings, but they are Sadducees to the backbone.

"*The cynicism of the official who feared not God nor regarded man, administered justice in our Lord's instance from mere annoyance. For him justice has no majesty and the misfortune of the widow had no sacredness. That which he could not be got to do, either for the fear of God or out of regard to man, he yet hastened to do merely to save himself from annoyance; and this is a thoroughly Sadducean trait*" (Stalker). (See Luke 18:1-8.)

The spirit of "I do not wish to be annoyed" is frequently the inspiration of the administration of justice in private cases. It works into our intercession also: I want that bad person saved—because he is of so much value in the sight of

God? No, because he is an annoyance to me, I cannot live my life properly with him. That spirit cannot live anywhere near Jesus Christ, because Jesus had only one point of view—His Father's will.

In any work I do for God is my motive loyalty to Jesus, or do I have to stop and wonder where He comes in? If I work for God because I know it brings me the good opinion of those whose good opinion I wish to have, I am a Sadducee. The one great thing is to maintain a spiritual life which is absolutely true to Jesus Christ and to the faith of Jesus Christ.

The Base Impulse (Continued)

Lord, Lord, when we are dead, remember not
All our lost sorrows and our soul's endeavor,
Better to bear the burden of our lot,
Firmer to stand how strong the storm so-ever,
Only remember all the agony
Thou bearest in the Garden silently.

And when the soul by death is freed again,
Thou wilt not let the rapture of her wings
Be marred by memory of this life's pain,
But lift our hearts above our sufferings
Lord, let our soul's life after all these years
Rise stronger, wiser, cleaner for its tears.

(1) *The Low Man with a Little Thing To Do*

The base impulse is the way sin works into our minds and gives us a totally wrong view of God. If the base impulse does not show itself in flesh and blood sins, it will show itself in mean-mindedness. Try to imagine what Jesus meant when He said, "Preach the gospel to every creature"; He keeps "an open house" for the whole universe. It is a conception impossible of human comprehension.

(a) Moral Distinctions. We are interested in other men's lives because of a career, a profession, or an ideal we have for them, but God does not seem to care an atom for careers or professions, He comes down with ruthless disregard of all gifts and geniuses and sweeps them on one side; He is inter-

ested only in one thing, and that thing was exhibited in the life of our Lord—a balanced holiness before God. Our Lord's character is the full-orbed expression of God's ideal of a human being. We can never take any one virtue and say Jesus Christ was the representative of that virtue; we cannot speak of Jesus Christ being a holy Man or a great Man or a good Man; Jesus Christ cannot be summed up in terms of natural virtues, but only in terms of the supernatural. If we can describe a man by any one virtue, he ceases to be God's idea of a man, and the characteristic of the Spirit of God in us is that He brings us "to the measure of the stature of the fullness of Christ."

(b) *Money Matters and the Master's Mind.*

"Money is the sign and symbol of all earthly possessions; it is earthly pleasure in a solid condition, only requiring to be melted to assume any of its more volatile and usable forms; and the pursuit of it easily becomes an absorbing passion even with those who have forgotten how to turn it into these equivalents. On this subject the language of Jesus is astonishingly severe" (Stalker).

Jesus saw in money a much more formidable enemy of the kingdom of God than we are apt to recognize it to be. Money is one of the touchstones of reality. People say, "We must lay up for a rainy day." We must, if we do not know God. How many of us are willing to go the length of Jesus Christ's teaching? Ask yourself, how does the advocacy of insurance agree with the Sermon on the Mount, and you will soon see how un-Christian we are in spite of all our Christian jargon. The more we try to reconcile modern principles of economy with the teachings of Jesus, the more we shall have to disregard Jesus. Whenever we read anything that is very plain in our Lord's words, we either say that we cannot understand it or that it has another meaning.

Common sense is the best gift we have, but it must be under the dominant rule of God. We enthrone common sense, we do not enthrone God. People must reason according to their god, and the god of today is common sense; that is why Jesus Christ's teaching is ruled out of court. If we try to apply the principles of the Sermon on the Mount to ordinary business life today, we shall see where we are. Civilization was founded by a murderer, and the very soul and genius of civilization is competition. What we are trying to do today is to Christianize civilization, and our social problems exist because Jesus Christ's teaching is being ruled out.

(2) The High Man with a Great Thing To Do

"Profound as is His sense of the wickedness of the world and the lostness of the individual, the ground-tone of His preaching is not despair, but hope, and the final and enduring impression left on the mind by the prolonged and sympathetic study of all His words is, that there is an essence of divine dignity and immeasurable value, which it is the task of the Savior and of all who are inspired with His aims to rescue from the dangers to which it is exposed and to redeem to a destiny of blessedness and immortality" (Stalker).

(a) *Solidarity of Sin.* Solidarity means oneness of interest. We are familiar with the phrase "the solidarity of the human race," but there is also a solidarity of sin (a oneness of interest in sin), and a solidarity of salvation (a oneness of interest in salvation). I mean by sin, not sin in a particular sense, but in the great big general sense which means a violation or neglect of the laws of morality or religion, and God's Book shows that there is a oneness of interest in all sin. The psalms show a wonderful discrimination about sin (see 32:2); they refer to the same thing the apostle Paul refers to in Ephesians 6:12—the supernatural inspiration of sin.

We have considered the three great sins of our Lord's day—the sin of the publican, of the Pharisee, and of the Sadducee—and now we must look to the fact that our Lord considered men as evil. "If you, then, being evil . . ." (Luke 11:13). Jesus Christ is made to teach the opposite of this by modern teachers; they make out that He taught the goodness of human nature. Jesus Christ revealed that men were evil, and that He came that He might plant in them the very nature that was in Himself. He cannot, however, begin to do this until a man recognizes himself as Jesus sees him.

We start with the idea that some people are good and some bad; but we are all bad, everyone of us needs saving by Jesus Christ. Imagine that being believed today! We can hear Christendom saying, "Nonsense, human nature is not evil."

The feature of today is the love of people who hate God. We are alienated from the standpoint of Jesus, we have become incarnated by a leaven that never came from His point of view, and if we are going to stand for Him we shall find that what He said is true. "They will turn you out of the synagogues"—not because we denounce sin, a socialist denounces sin as much as a preacher of the gospel. The difference between a Christian worker and one who does not know Jesus Christ is just this—that a Christian worker can never meet anyone of whom he can despair. If we do despair of anyone, it is because we have never met Jesus Christ ourselves. The social worker who does not know what Jesus Christ came to do will end in absolute despair before long, because the social worker more than anyone else begins to see the enormous havoc that sin has made of human nature, and if he does not know the Savior from sin, all his efforts will meet with as much success as attempting to empty the Atlantic Ocean with a thimble.

(b) Savior from Sin. The great challenge in personal work is—What relationship have I to Jesus Christ? It is not simply that we realize the power of Jesus to save, but that we recognize the possibilities for evil in our own heart, discerned in us by the Holy Spirit, and know that Jesus can save unto the uttermost. Let a man be a murderer, or an evildoer, or any of the things Jesus said men could be, it can never shake our confidence if we have once been face to face with Jesus Christ for ourselves. It is impossible to discourage us because we start from a knowledge of who Jesus Christ is in our own life. When we see evil and wrong exhibited in other lives, instead of awakening a sickening despair, it awakens a joyful confidence—I know a Savior who can save even that one. One worker like that is of priceless worth, because through that one life the Son of God is being manifested.

It is not only necessary to have an experience of God's grace, we must have a body of beliefs alive with the Spirit of Jesus, then when we have learned to see people as He sees them, there is no form of disease or anguish or devilishness that can belch up in human life that can disturb our confidence in Him; if it does disturb us, it is because we don't know Him.

The sense of sin is in inverse ratio to its presence, that is, the higher up and the deeper down we are saved, the more pangingly terrible is our conviction of sin. The holiest person is not the one who is not conscious of sin, but the one who is most conscious of what sin is. The one who talked most about sin was our Lord Jesus Christ. We are apt to run off with the idea that a man in order to be saved from sin must have lived a vile life himself; but the One who has an understanding of the awful horror of sin is the spotless holy Christ, Who "knew no sin." The lower down we get into the experience of sin, the less conviction of sin we have. When we are regenerated and lifted into the light, we begin to know what sin means. There is no mention of sin in the apostle Paul's apprehension by Christ, yet no one wrote more about sin than the apostle Paul years after in his Epistles, because by the marvelous working of God's grace and his own repentance, he was lifted into the heavenly places where he saw what sin really was. The danger with those of us who have experienced God's perfect salvation is that we talk blatant jargon about an experience instead of banking on the tremendous revelation of God the Holy Spirit. The purer we are through God's sovereign grace, the more terribly poignant is our sense of sin. It is perilous to say, "I have nothing to do with sin now"; you are the only kind of person who can know what sin is. Those living in sin don't know anything about it. Sin destroys the capacity of knowing what sin is. It is when we have been delivered from sin that we begin to realize by the pure light of the Holy Spirit what sin is. We shall find over and over again that God will send us shuddering to our knees every time we realize what sin is, and instead of it increasing hardness in us towards the men and women who are living in sin, the Spirit of God will use it as a means of bringing us to the dust before Him in vicarious intercession that God will save them as He has saved us. Beware of the metallic, hard, un-Christlike stamp of some testimonies to sanctification, they are not stamped by the Holy Spirit. The testimony to sanctification that is of God is dipped and saturated in the blood of the Son of God, and that blood sprang from the broken heart of God on account of sin. When once the soul realizes what sanctification is, it is a joy unspeakable, but it is a joy in which there is the tremendous undercurrent of a chastening humiliation. Beware of any experience that is not built absolutely on the atoning merit of Jesus Christ; and remember, the measure of your freedom from sin is the measure of your sense of what sin is.

YOUR GREAT REDEMPTION

Foreword

Writing in the War years (1917) Oswald Chambers said, "Through this war there will emerge new statements of God and of Christ. To me there emerge two or three grand facts: First, fathomless redemption as the basis of human life; absolute God-like forgiveness of sin; with a liberty to reject that basis on the part of man. Second, that God's name is Jesus Christ; not that He is a revelation from God, but that He is God. That means that God became the weakest thing in His creation—a babe. Third, that He can introduce into any man the heredity of the Son of God by new birth, in which His nature becomes operative in human nature, along with a series of educational developments." These articles on redemption contribute to that very end. "Everything that has been touched by sin and the devil has been redeemed; we are to live in the world immovably banked on that faith." What sure ground for our feet we have in that glorious truth as we stand for Jesus Christ, witnesses unto Him. But the in-working of redemption in personal life is grandly brought out in these living messages. I quote another sentence, "Immediately I accept the cross of Christ as the revelation of redemption I am not, I must not be, the same man; I must be another man, and I must take up my cross for my Lord." So we see redemption working inwardly, with our reactions to it, and with the resultant issues regarding sin and righteousness and judgment. The book is *more* than worth its weight in gold.

DAVID LAMBERT

Redemption

(1) Redemption in Realized Revelation (John 19:30).

We can never expound the redemption, but we must have strong unshaken faith in it so that we are not swept off our feet by actual things. That the devil and humankind are allowed to do as they like is a mere episode in the providence of God. Everything that has been touched by sin and the devil has been redeemed; we are to live in the world immovably banked in that faith. Unless we have faith in the redemption, all our activities are fussy impertinences which tell God He is doing nothing. We destroy our souls serving Jesus Christ, instead of abiding in Him. Jesus Christ is not working out the redemption; it is complete; we are working it out, and beginning to realize it by obedience. Our practical life is to be molded by our belief in the redemption, and our declared message will be in accordance with our belief. If we say we believe "It is finished" we must not blaspheme God by unbelief in any domain of our practical life.

We must make a distinction in our minds between the revelation of redemption and conscious participation in it. When we are born again we consciously enter into participation of the redemption. We do not help God to redeem the world; we realize that God has redeemed it. Redemption is not dependent on our experience of it. The human race is redeemed; we have to be so faithful to God that through us may come the awakening of those who have not yet realized that they are redeemed.

(2) Revelation and Redemption in Relation (2 Corinthians 5:18-21).

A sinner knows what the redemption has wrought in him, but it is only long afterwards that he begins to grasp the revelation of how that redemption was made particularly and in detail possible in him. It is one thing to be saved by God's grace, but another thing to have a clear revelation as to how God did it. Our Lord Jesus Christ is the revelation complete; the Bible is the revelation come down to the shores of our life in words. The grace of God can never alter; redemption can never alter; and the evidence that we are experiencing the grace of God in redemption is that it is manifestly working out in us in actual ways. When the words of the Bible come home to us by the Holy Spirit, the supernatural essence of the redemption is in those words and they bring forth new life in us. If you have been saved from sin, say so; if you have been sanctified by God's grace, say so. By using other words you are not testifying to God, but compromising with the atmosphere of those to whom you are talking.

The religion of Jesus Christ is not a religion of ethical truth, but of redemption. The teachings of Jesus have not made so much difference to the world as the teachings of Socrates and Plato, but to those who are born from above they make all the difference. The thing that tells is not that the actual life is lived rightly, but that the motive underneath is right. The characteristic of the redemption when it works out subjectively in accordance with Scripture is that act of devotion of Mary of Bethany. It was not useful, nor was it her duty; it was an extravagant waste, but the motive of it was the spontaneous originality which sprang from a personal passionate devotion to Jesus Christ. When a man has been profoundly moved in his spirit by the experience of redemption, then out of him flow rivers of living water. Stop the concern of whether you are of any use in the world. "He who believes in me," said Jesus, "out of him shall flow rivers of living water"; whether we see it or not is a matter of indifference. Heed the Source.

(3) *Redemption in Objective Form (Luke 24:44-47).*

The disciples after the resurrection received into themselves an influx from the risen Christ—"their eyes were opened and they knew Him" (24:31); and their minds were opened, "that they might understand the Scriptures" (24:45). The characteristic of being born again is that we know who Jesus is. The secret of the Christian is that he knows the absolute deity of the Lord Jesus Christ. When we are saved by God's grace our minds are opened by the incoming of the Holy Spirit and we understand the Scriptures. The test of regeneration is that the Bible instantly becomes the Book of books to us.

The objective form of the redemption comes to us through the person of the Lord Jesus Christ, and works itself out in saving judgments. The bedrock of Christianity is repentance. There is a certain type of badness that exhausts itself, and the nature is righted by ordinary hereditary reactions, and that is frequently mistaken for the regenerating work of God. If it is the work of the Spirit of God, repentance is its basis. We can only test the experimental working of redemption by the fruits the New Testament has taught us to expect. "Therefore bear fruits worthy of repentance" (Luke 3:8).

Redemption:
The Christian's Greatest Trust

(1) The Cross and the Father's Heart
(John 12:28; Galatians 6:14)

We can understand the attributes of God in other ways, but we can only understand the Father's heart in the cross of Christ. The cross of Christ is not the cross of a martyr, it has become the symbol of the martyr; it is the revelation of redemption. The cross is the crystalized point in history where eternity merges with time. The cry on the cross, "My God, My God, why have You forsaken Me?" is not the desolation of an isolated individual; it is the revelation of the heart of God face to face with the sin of the human race, and going deeper down than people's sin can ever go in unconceivable heartbreak that every sin-stained, hell-deserving sinner might be absolutely redeemed. If the redemption of Christ cannot go deeper down than hell, it is not redemption at all.

It is always the tragic note that is struck when once the Spirit of God gets hold of a person. The reason we are so shallow and flippant in our presentation of the cross is that we have never seen ourselves for one second in the light of God. When we do see ourselves in the light of God, there is only one of two refuges—suicide or the cross of Christ. The great condemnation of much of our modern preaching is that it conveys no sense of the desperate tragedy of conviction of sin. When once the real touch of conviction of sin comes, it is hell on earth—there is no other word for it. One second of realizing ourselves in the light of God means unspeakable agony and distress; but the marvel is that when the conviction does come, there is God in the very center of the whole thing to save us from it. That is the meaning of the cross of Christ as experimentally applied to us. We have to face ourselves with the revelation of the redemption, mirrored and concentrated in the cross of Jesus Christ as it is presented in the New Testament, before we get the shallow, pious nonsense shaken out of our religious beliefs. To be saved by God's grace is not a beautifully pathetic thing; it is a desperately tragic thing.

(2) *The Cross and the Savior's Mind (Matthew 16:24; Galatians 2:20).*

The evidence that I have accepted the cross of Christ as the revelation of redemption is that the regenerating life of God is manifested in my mortal flesh. Immediately I accept the cross of Christ as the revelation of redemption I am not, I must not be, the same man, I must be another man, and I must take up my cross from my Lord. The cross is the gift of Jesus to His disciples and it can only bear one aspect: "I am not my own." The whole attitude of the life is that I have given up my right to myself. I live like a crucified man. Unless that crisis is reached it is perilously possible for my religious life to end as a sentimental fiasco. "I don't mind being saved from hell and receiving the Holy Spirit, but it is too much to expect me to give up my right to myself to Jesus Christ, to give up my manhood, my womanhood, all my ambitions." Jesus said, If any man will be My disciple, those are the conditions. It is that kind of thing that offended the historic disciples, and it will offend you and me. It is a slander to the cross of Christ to say we believe in Jesus and please ourselves all the time, choosing our own way.

Our salvation is one of unspeakable freedom for heart and mind and body, but do we sufficiently brood on what it cost God to make it ours? At certain stages of Christian experience a saint has no courtesy toward God, no sense of gratitude; he is thankful for being delivered from sin, but the thought of living for Jesus, of being recklessly abandoned to Him, has not begun to dawn on him yet. When we come to the cross we do not go through it and out the other side; we abide in the life to which the cross is the gateway, and the characteristic of the life is that of deep profound sacrifice to God. Social service that is not based on the cross of Christ is the cultured blasphemy of civilized life against God, because it denies that God has done anything, and puts human effort as the only way whereby the world will be redeemed.

Relative Redemptive Reactions

An abiding snare in dealing with Christian doctrine arises from the tendency to bend the attention exclusively either to the objective or the subjective side. If we deal only with the objective, it produces the type of practical life that contradicts the creed believed in; and to deal only with the subjective side produces the moody, sickly introspective type of life, its eyes fixed on its own whiteness. The wholesome antidote to either tendency is the New Testament, which embraces both the objective and the subjective through the miracle of regeneration. Belief in the New Testament is always practical and positive, that is, it instantly manifests itself. I do not "gull" myself into believing something has happened; it is a fact; I am not only right with God but am actually proving that I am in my life. If my faith in the redemptive work of Christ does not react in a practical life which manifests it, the reason is a wrong temper of mind in me.

How ought life from the ascended Lord to react in me? by reaction is meant not a reaction of nerves but the essential nature of the life. The danger of dealing only with the objective side is that it blinds our minds to the fact that we have to receive something which must have a reaction, "to open their eyes, . . . that they may receive" (Acts 26:18). That means the will of the individual is willing to receive. Not only has Jesus Christ been seen and believed in, but accepted, and the reaction in the life is as radical as the stupendous miracle that made it possible.

(1) Sympathies—Humanitarian or Evangelical (Galatians 3:6).

If I feel sympathy with anyone because he cannot get through to God, I am slandering God; my fundamental view is not the evangelical one, but a point of view based on mere human sympathy. Trace where your sympathies arise, and be sympathetic with God, never with the soul who finds it difficult to get through to God. God is never to blame. "Remember the people." Don't! Remember the Christ who saves you. We are not here to woo and win people to God; we are here to present the gospel which in individual cases will mean condemnation or salvation. "Where you get the most faithful preaching, you get the most hardened sinners" (Thos. Guthrie). It is perilous to listen to the truth of God unless I open my will to it. We have not to rouse people's sympathies and humanitarian conceptions—"How beautiful and dignified man is!" We have rigorously to push an issue of will, and when the issue is put you find the obstruction; people resent it, and that is the barrier to God. Immediately that barrier is down God comes in like a torrent, there is nothing to keep Him back; the one thing that keeps Him back is anarchy and rebellion, the essential nature of Satan—I won't give up my right to myself; I won't yield, and God is powerless. Immediately a man removes the barriers it is as if God romped into his soul with all His almightiness; it is a flood of blessing quite overwhelming.

(2) Strenuousness—Holy or Evangelistic (2 Corinthians 6:1-2).

Jesus Christ is not an individual who died twenty centuries ago; He is God and mankind centered in His cross. The cross is the revelation of the deepest depth in Almighty God. What should be the reaction of that in my life?

Holiness, rugged, fierce holiness in every detail of the life. That is the meaning of New Testament repentance. The only truly repentant man is the holy man, he has been made holy through the incoming of God by his willing reception of Him. Evangelistic effort must never forget the source from which it springs; it often does, and all that is presented is the objective side which has no practical outcome in the life.

(3) Sacrifices—Homely or Extraordinary (Luke 14:26-27, 33)

These are extraordinary sacrifices, they cut clean across everything we believe naturally. We must have the marks in our hands and feet that are exactly like Our Lord's. There must be the crucified love of grasp for myself; the crucified love of wandering in my own ways; the crucified love of the world; the wounded pride of intellect. There is no bigger word and no word made more shallow than "surrender." To say "I surrender all" may be blathering sentiment, or it may be the deep passionate utterance of the life.

(4) Strongholds—Honest or Exceptional (Acts 20:24)

Actions that spring from obedience to Jesus Christ can never be explained on any other ground. This is where the "shame" of testifying comes in. Testimony is not a hard protestation that I have done something better than others, nor is it first a means of helping others; it means that I have ventured out on God and have no one to rely upon but Him. I have staked my all in obedience to Jesus Christ in this matter, and it is sink or swim. Try to explain why you did a certain thing; if it sprang from obedience to Christ, and you find you cannot. It is not the logical working out of a principle, and that is why the other relationships of life do not see it. "If anyone comes to Me and does not hate his father and mother, . . . he cannot be My disciple." Remember, the crisis may never come to you, and instead of the claims of father or mother clashing with the commands of Jesus Christ, you may be clashing with the commands of His coming to you through them. But if the crisis does arise, it must be prompt obedience to Jesus Christ at every cost.

"The Lord God Omnipotent Reigns"

To believe that the Lord God omnipotent reigns and redeems is the end of all possible panic, moral, intellectual or spiritual. We say we believe God, and give the lie to it with every breath we draw. For a person to believe in the redemption means that no crime nor terror nor anguish can discourage him, no matter where he is placed. God is not saving the world; it is done, our business is to get men and women to realize it, and we cannot do it unless we realize it ourselves.

(1) Redemptive Sanctuary (Jeremiah 17:12).

"What needs doing is all less than has been done. What has to be done for the world is already done in God" (Dr. Forsyth).

We can do nothing for the redemption of the world; we have to do in the world that which proves we believe it is redeemed; all our activities are based on that unshakable knowledge, therefore we are never distressed out of that sanctuary. God make us go a solitary way until we get there, but through one life that is there, comes all the force of the redemption. The thing that makes our hearts fail is the profound disbelief on the part of Christian workers that God has done anything, and the wearing out of life to do what is already done. All the fuss and energy and work that goes on if we are not believing in Jesus Christ and His redemption, has not a touch of the almighty power of God about it; it is a panic of unbelief veneered over with Christian phrases. As long as we pretend to be believers in Jesus Christ and are not, we produce humbugs, and people say, "Do you call that Christianity? There is nothing in it!" or what is worse, we produce frauds, and the worst type of fraud is the religious fraud. The greatest type of reality is the Christian believer—one who has been totally readjusted on the basis of his belief. When you come across a believer in Jesus, his very presence alters your outlook. It is not that you have come to someone with amazing intelligence, but that you have come into a sanctuary which is based on a real knowledge of the redemption. When once a man really believes that the world is redeemed, his belief will manifest itself in every detail, and that is what constitutes the heroism of a believer in Jesus Christ. Our skepticism arises from the fact that we have no experimental knowledge of redemption.

(2) *Redemptive Secret (Philippians 3:13-14).*

Our Christian destiny is to fulfill "the high calling of God in Christ Jesus." When a soul comes face to face with God, the eternal redemption of the Lord Jesus is concentrated in that little microcosm of an individual life, and through the pinhole of that one life other people can see the whole landscape of God's purpose. The point is, am I realizing the redemption in my home circle, among my friends, in the pecuniary circumstances I am in? It is not heroism that makes us sacrifice ourselves, but cowardice; we can't stand being considered cads for not sacrificing ourselves. That is the basis of much of the sacrifice made in the world. The believer is one who bases all on Jesus Christ's sacrifice, and is so identified with Him that he is made broken bread and poured-out wine in the hands of his Lord. "Witnesses to Me," a satisfaction to Jesus Christ wherever we are placed. When once we get to the right center of energy, the omnipotence of God is at work all the time.

(3) Redemptive Satisfaction (John 3:16).

We reason in this way: "God is so loving that I know He will forgive me." God is so holy that it is much more likely he will say I must be damned. Unless God can alter me He dare not forgive me; if He did I should have a keener sense of justice and right than He has. The realization of the nature of God's love produces in me the convulsions of repentance, and repentance fully worked out means holiness, a radical adjustment of the life. Do I know God has saved me? Have I the satisfaction of that salvation? I can easily know whether the redemption has been made efficacious in me by the Holy Spirit by the fact that I am at one with God. The redemption is worked out in an at-one-ment with God, in every calculation He is the One who dominates everything.

The assurance of faith is a certainty more certain than certainty, and it always comes with an experimental knowledge of the redemption. Belief in the redemption is difficult because it needs surrender first. I never can believe until I have surrendered myself to God. "If any one wills to do His will,"—what is His will? "That you believe on Him whom He has sent."

The Ruling Issues of Redemption

John 16:7-15

"And when He has come, He will convict the world of sin, and of righteousness, and of judgment."

The word *convict* means moral conviction, not logical conviction. When the Holy Spirit is come, He will convict a man with a power of moral conviction beyond the possibility of getting away from it. Whenever the Holy Spirit gets us into a corner, He never convinces our intellect; He is busy with the will which expresses itself in our intellect. It is never safe to do much introspection, but it is ruinous to do none. Introspection can never satisfy us, yet introspection is not wrong, it is right, because it is the only way we discover that we need God. It is the introspective power in us that is made alert by conviction of sin.

(1) The Issue Regarding Sin. *"Of sin, because they do not believe in Me."*

Note what causes you the deepest concern before God. Does social evil produce a deeper concern than the fact that people do not believe on Jesus Christ? It was not social evil that brought Jesus Christ down from heaven, it was the great primal sin of independence of God that brought God's Son to Calvary. Sin is not measured by a law or by a social standard, but by a person. The Holy Spirit is unmistakable in His working: *"And when He has come, He will convict the world of sin, and of righteousness, and of judgment, . . . because they do not believe in Me."*

That is the very essence of sin. The Holy Spirit brings moral conviction on that line, and on no other. A man does not need the Holy Spirit to tell him that external sins are wrong, ordinary culture and education will do that; but it does take the Holy Spirit to convict us of sin as our Lord defined it—*"Because they do not believe in Me."* Sin is not measured by a standard of moral rectitude and uprightness, but by my relationship to Jesus Christ. The point is, am I morally convinced that the only sin there is in the sight of the Holy Spirit, is disbelief in Jesus?

(2) The Issue Regarding Righteousness. *"Of righteousness, because I go to My Father."*

If I am not morally convinced with regard to sin, I won't bother my head about Jesus Christ going to the Father and having all power in heaven and on earth; but once I am convicted of sin, and have accepted deliverance from unbelief in Jesus, I know beyond the shadow of a doubt that Jesus Christ is the Righteous One. The wisdom of God is shown in that Jesus Christ was made unto us righteousness . . . (1 Corinthians 1:30). That means that God can justly justify the unjust and remain righteous. In the cross of Calvary our Lord is revealed as the Just One making men just before God. God never justifies men outside Christ. No man can stand for one second on any right or justice of his own; but as he abides in Christ, Jesus Christ is made righteousness unto him (see Philippians 3:8-9). Today the tendency is to switch away from "the righteousness which is of God by faith," and to put the emphasis on doing things. You cannot do anything at all that does not become, in the rugged language of Isaiah, "as filthy rags," if it is divorced from living faith in Jesus Christ. If we have the tiniest hankering after believing we can be justified by what we have done, we are on the wrong side of the cross. To experience the loss of my own goodness is the only way to enter into communion with God in Christ (2 Corinthians 5:21).

(3) The Issue Regarding Judgment. "Of judgment, because the ruler of this world is judged."

Have I come to judgment at the foot of the cross? Do I accept God's verdict on sin given there? What one longs to see more often is a soul shattered under the convicting blast of the Holy Spirit. It means that Jesus Christ has seen of the travail of His soul in that one, and it is one of the rarest sights. Most of us are smugly satisfied with praising Jesus Christ without ever having realized what the cross means. We say, "O Lord, I want to be sanctified," and at any moment in answer to that prayer the Holy Spirit may rip and tear your conscience and stagger you dumb by conviction of sin, and the question is, will you accept God's verdict on sin on the cross of Christ, or will you whine and compromise? The only test of spirituality is holiness, practical, living holiness, and that holiness is impossible unless the Holy Spirit has brought you to your "last day," and you can look back and say—"That was the day when I died right out to my right to myself, crucified with Christ." That is the day from which many a rich young ruler and many a Mary of Bethany goes away sorrowful, with countenance fallen, for they have great possessions of self-respect, great possessions in the way of ideas as to how they want to serve God. The "last day" is when a soul, gripped by the power and light of the Holy Spirit, sees the meaning of the cross of Christ, and goes to death like a sentenced criminal. To every soul who has gone through that experience, there is "no more condemnation" (Romans 8:1).

The Character of Redeemed Experience

By redeemed experience is meant eternal life manifested in the fleeting moments of temporal life. What is not meant is the consciousness of feeling good, or the consciousness of the presence of God. If we mistake these feelings for eternal life, we shall be disillusioned sooner or later. When we are being initiated into a new experience we are conscious of it, but any sane person is much too wise to mistake consciousness of life for life itself. It is only the initial stages of new experiences which produce consciousness of themselves, and if we hug the consciousness of God's blessings and of His presence we become spiritual sentimentalists. God began to introduce us to life, and we would not go through with it.

(1) The Unique Character of This Life (John 6:47).

What is eternal life? "And this is eternal life, that they may know You the only true God" (John 17:3). "Eternal" has reference to the quality of the life. Our Lord says very distinctly what eternal life is not (see Matthew 4:4; Luke 12:15). Whenever our Lord speaks of "life" He means eternal life, and He says, "You have no life in you" (John 6:53). People have natural life and intellectual life apart from Jesus Christ.

The life that Jesus Christ exhibited was eternal life, and He says—anyone who believes in Me, that is, commits himself to Me, has that life. To commit myself to Jesus means there is nothing that is not committed. Belief is a twofold transaction—a deliberate destroying of all roads back again, and a complete surrender to our Lord Himself. God comes in with a rush immediately a soul surrenders to the Lord Jesus Christ. The only barrier to God's love is unbelief working sentimentally—brooding around the shores of an experience which produces consciousness of itself; the life is not there.

(2) The Upward Character of the Life (John 11:41-42).

The upward look toward God of eternal life is an indication of the inherent nature of the life; that is, it is not attained by effort. Natural characteristics, natural virtues and natural attainments have nothing to do with the life itself. A blackguard and an upright man both commit themselves to Jesus Christ and receive eternal life; will the latter have freer access to God? No! Eternal life works the same in both. There is no respect of persons with God. The manifestation of eternal life is, however, a different matter.

(3) The Outward Character of the Life (John 3:16).

This verse gives the outlook manward of eternal life as exhibited in our Lord. The only way to react rightly on men around is to let eternal life react through you, and if you want to know how eternal life will react you will see it in Jesus Christ. Our Lord was in no wise a hard worker; He was an intense reality. Hard workers are like midges and mosquitoes; the reality is like the mountain and the lake. Our Lord's life was one of amazing leisure, and the presentation of His life as one of rush is incorrect. The three years of public life are a manifestation of the intense reality of life (Acts 10:38). When the passion for souls obscures the passion for Jesus Christ you have the devil on your track as an angel of light. Our Lord was never in a hurry, never in a panic. "There are no dates in His fine leisure." Our Lord's life is the exhibition of eternal life in time. Eternal life in the Christian is based on redemptive certainty; he is not working to redeem men; he is a fellow worker with God among men because they are redeemed.

(4) *The Downward Character of This Life (2 Corinthians 5:21).*

The downward look of eternal life is manifested by our Lord—a fearless, clear-eyed, understanding look at sin, at death, and at the devil—that is the unmistakable characteristic of the downward look of our Lord. The devil's counterfeit is no sin, no hell, and no judgment.

The Magnitude of Redemption

1 Thessalonians 5:23

We cannot be deeply moved by "nothing"; neither can we deeply move ourselves by anything we say, unless something profound has first of all entered into us. For example, it takes a great deal of realizing what the Bible reveals about redemption to enable us to walk out into our daily lives with that astonishing strength and peace that garrisons us within and without.

(1) The Working of Redemptive Security. "May the God of peace Himself sanctify you completely."

The working of redemptive security in our actual practical life is the realization that "God is my Father, I shall never think of anything He will forget—why should I worry?" When you can say that from the ground of being profoundly moved, you are astonished at the amazing security. "My peace I give to you" (John 14:27). The peace of Christ is synonymous with His very nature, and the "type" working of that peace was exhibited in our Lord's earthly life. "The peace of God, which surpasses all understanding..." (Philippians 4:7). The redemption at work in my actual life means the nature of God garrisoning me round; it is the God of peace who sanctifies wholly; the security is almighty. The gift of the peace of Christ on the inside; the garrison of God on the outside, then I have to see that I allow the peace of God to regulate all that I do, that is where my responsibility comes in—"And let the peace of Christ rule," that is, arbitrate, "in your hearts," and life will be full of praise all the time.

(2) *The Working of Redemptive Strength.* "*And may your whole spirit, soul, and body . . . .*"

The degree in which God will work depends on me, not on God; if I refuse in any part of my being to let God work, I not only limit Him, but I begin to criticize the redemption. The working of redemptive strength means that "all spiritual blessings in heavenly places" are mine when I am "at home" with God. Take up your dwelling in that word, *all*, then do some hunting through the Bible for spiritual blessings and say, "That is mine." If you remain on the outside and say, "Lord, bless me with this spiritual blessing," He cannot do it; the only result is to make you feel miserable. But get inside Christ, and all spiritual blessings in heavenly places are yours. It is not a question of experiencing them, you don't experience what is your life; you experience gifts given to your life. Experiences are always on the threshold of the life, they are never the real center. Life is fullness of maturity, and there is no seeking for experiences. Beware of not seeing that experiences are nothing other than gateways home. "Saved and sanctified"—Paul says, "Go on! Get into the heavenly places in Christ Jesus." You will be so hidden with Christ that you never think of anything but Him; there will be none of the things that keep the life impoverished.

(3) *The Working Redemptive Safety.* "*Be preserved blameless . . .*"

"He who dwells in the secret place of the Most High shall abide under the shadow of the Almighty." Dwelling under that shadow I am in the heart of Almighty God;

where I dwell He manifests Himself all the time. It is an essentially natural life. When I am dwelling under the shadow of the Almighty, my life is the will of God; it is only through disobedience that I begin to ask what is the will of God. Any interest that would induce me away from the shadow of the Almighty is to be treated as a snare. Resolutely treat no one seriously but God. "The LORD is my rock and my fortress and my deliverer; my God, my strength . . . my shield and the horn of my salvation, my stronghold" (Psalm 18:2). Note the "my's" here, and laugh at everything in the nature of misgiving for ever after!

(4) The Working of Redemptive Sight. "Be preserved blameless at the coming [presence] of our Lord Jesus Christ."

The working of redemptive sight gives me the habit of an elevated mood whereby God gives the vision of Himself. "Blessed are the pure in heart," literally, "Blessed are the God in heart," that is, in whom the nature of God is. God's nature in us reveals His features in our life. "Man shall not see Me and live." When I see God I have to die; when I am in God I have died, and the nature of God works through me transparently all the time. "We know that, if He shall be manifested, we shall be like Him; for we shall see Him even as He is."

The only way to maintain perception is to keep in contact with God's purpose as well as with His person. I have to place myself in relation to facts—facts in nature and facts in grace. If I refuse to do this my perception will be wrong, no matter how right my disposition may be; but the two working together will produce a life perfectly in accordance with the life of the Son of God when he walked this earth.

"God is able to make all grace abound toward you."

Have you been saying, "I cannot expect God to do that for me? Why can't you? Is God Almighty impoverished by your circumstances? Is His hand shortened that it cannot save? Are your particular circumstances so peculiar, so remote from the circumstances of every son and daughter of Adam, that the atonement and the grace of God are not sufficient for you? Immediately we ask ourselves these things, we get shaken out of our sulks into a simple trust in God. When we have the simple, childlike trust in God that Jesus exhibited, the overflowing grace of God will have no limits, and we must set no limits to it.

Actually Born into Redemption

John 3:4

The abiding reality is God, and He makes known His order in the fleeting moments. Redemption partakes of God's character, therefore it is not fleeting; but we have the power and the privilege of exhibiting the redemption in the fleeting moments of our actual life. This is the real meaning of being born from above. Civilization is based on principles which imply that the passing moment is permanent. The only permanent thing is God, and if I put anything else as permanent, I become atheistic. I must build only on God (John 14:6). "Because God spoke to me once, I stick to that." You are a fool if you do. Stick to the God who spoke to you. He is speaking the word all the time; it is only as we are trained by obedience that we can understand Him (John 6:63).

(1) The Standard of Actual Redemption.

This simply means the manifestation of the life of God in the actual fleeting moments of my life. The eternal reality of God's redemption is there all the time; being born from above means that I am partaking in it. Nicodemus' question, "How can a man be born when he is old?" (John 3:4) is an exhibition of cultured stupidity, which is denser than ignorant stupidity because it won't be enlightened. Immediately I ask "how can?" I evade the "you must." God never debates or argues.

"We know that whoever is born of God does not sin" (1 John 5:18). The life of God in me does not sin (see 1 John

3:9). If I am based on the redemption, this standard will manifest itself in the actual moments of my life—I must not sin. It is not something I set myself to do, but something I know I never can do, therefore I let God do it. "I know that in me (that is, in my flesh) nothing good dwells" (Romans 7:18). Born from above, I realize that the life of God has entered into me. God gives me "Himself," "The gift of God is eternal life" (Romans 6:23), and "eternal life" consciously in me is to know God (John 17:3). The life of God cannot commit sin, and if I will obey the life of God, which has come into me by regeneration, it will manifest itself in my mortal flesh. It is only when I disobey the life of God that I commit sin; then I must get back again into the light by confession (1 John 1:9). If I walk in the light as God is in the light, sin is not.

Actual redemption is as positive as real redemption. We never enter into the kingdom of God by having our head questions answered, but only by commitment.

(2) *Statement of Actual Recognition.*

Christ has to unsettle the certainty of a man's pagan mind; the wind of the Spirit touches him across the fleeting moments of his life, and he gets disturbed. The need, then, is for someone sure of Christ, and sure of His Word, to patiently watch for that soul, and that kind of watching is the meaning of intercession. The Holy Spirit imparts the energy of the redemption into human hearts by means of actual words, and it is to this that Peter refers in his epistle. "Having been born again, not of corruptible seed but incorruptible, through the word of God . . ." (1 Peter 1:23-25). Redemption comes to the shores of our human lives in actual words. "You must get a word from God." "Be sure you get the witness that this is so." The assurance is more positive than intellectual knowledge. The Spirit of God always works with the Word of God.

(3) Substance of Active Realization.

When a man is actually born from above, he knows that the redemption is as eternal as Almighty God. The disturbance by the Spirit of God opens one's eyes and he turns from darkness to light, from the authority of Satan to God; then he is ready to receive the Holy Spirit who conveys to him "forgiveness of sins and an inheritance among those who are sanctified . . ." (Acts 26:18). Receiving necessitates conscious poverty (see Matthew 20:22; Mark 14:50; John 20:22). Receiving in its elementary and in its complete stages is described in John 1:12-13, "But as many as received Him, to them gave He the right to become children of God, to those who believe in His name . . ." because to receive Jesus even intellectually, means that I commit myself. If I really receive Jesus Christ with my mind, I am given the right to become a son of God. The Holy Spirit makes that right an actual possession, and I receive sonship. To receive power to become a son of God means that I realize I am not a son; if I think I am a son already, I will patronize God. The at-one-ment means being made actually one with God through the redemption of our Lord. This is to receive a kingdom which cannot be shaken.

Dimensions of Effective Redemption

John 3:16; Ephesians 3:18-19

By "the dimensions of effective redemption," understand the redemption of God expressing itself in individual experience; but beware of limiting the redemption to our individual experience of it.

Breadth. "For God so loved the world..."

The world embraces things material and things evil, things suffering and sinning. Think how narrow and bigoted the love of God is made when it is tied up in less than His own words; we make God out to be exactly the opposite of all Jesus Christ said He was. The breadth of the love of God, the agony of that love, is expressed in one word, "so." If you can estimate the "so," you have fathomed the nature of God. Our love is defective because we will not get down low enough. We must get down lower than hell if we would touch the love of God; we will persist in living in the sixteenth story when the love of God is at the basement. We speculate on God's love, and discourse on the magnificence of the redemption, while all the time it has never been made effective in us.

> The love of God is broader
> Than the measures of man's mind

it embraces the whole world. Compare John 3:16 with our Lord's prayer in John 17. Our Lord did not pray that the world might be saved, but "that the world may know that You have . . . loved them." Our Lord prays for those in whom His redemption is at work that they may live in effective contact with God—"that they may be one, even as We are one."

The same thing with regard to sin and misery. In the Bible you never find the note of the pessimist. In the midst of the most crushing conditions there is always an extraordinary hopefulness and profound joy, because God is at the heart. The effective working of redemption in our experience makes us leap for joy in the midst of things in which other people see nothing but disastrous calamity. When the redemption is effectually at work it always rises to its source, namely, God.

Length. "*That He gave His only begotten Son . . .*"

When the supreme love of God in the giving of Himself has gotten hold of me, I love myself in the power of His love; that means a son of God being presented to God as a result of His effectual redemption. "Bringing many sons to glory . . ." (Hebrews 2:10). That is a gratification to God because it is the returning back to Himself of His love in expressed reality. When the redemption is effective in me, I am a delight to God, not to myself. I am not meant for myself, I am meant for God.

Depth. "*That whoever believes in Him should not perish . . .*"

The love of God rakes the very bottom of hell, and from the depths of sin and suffering brings sons and daughters to God. To introduce the idea of merit into belief, that is, that I have dome something by believing, is to annul my belief and make it blasphemous. Belief is the abandonment of all claim to desert; that is why it is so difficult to believe in Jesus. It requires the renunciation of the idea that I am someone—"I must have this thing explained to me;" "I must be convinced first." When the Spirit of God gets hold of me, He takes the foundation of the fictitious out of me and leaves nothing but an aching cavern for God to fill. "Blessed are the poor in spirit."

We love the lovely because it is flattering to us to do so. We love our kith and kin because it is the economy of pride to do so. God loves the unlovely, and it broke His heart to do it. The depth of the love of God is revealed by that wonderful word "whosoever." The Bible reveals God to be the Lover of His enemies (Romans 5:6-10). We will stick to our "rag rights," until by God's engineering of our circumstances, every "rag right" is blown from us and we are left with nothing; we become abject paupers, and say, "It's all up," and we find ourselves in heaven! We will persist in sticking to the thing that must be damned.

> Not by wrestling, but by clinging,
> Shall we be most blessed.

Height. "But have everlasting life."

The redemption of Jesus Christ effectively at work in me puts me where He was, and where He is, and where we shall forever be (John 16:23, 26; 14:23). It is the terrific lift by the sheer, unaided love of God into a precious oneness with Himself, if I will only let Him do it. It is not a magic-working thing, but the energy of His own life. The "realest" thing is the love of God by means of the effective working of redemption. On the human plane we may have love real, but low; my love, that is, the sovereign preference of my person for another person, is in order that my purpose may be fulfilled; and when Jesus Christ comes into the life, it looks as if He were the dead enemy of that love. He is not; He is the dead enemy of the lowness. When the love of God is realized by me, the sovereign preference of my person for God enables Him to manifest His purpose in me.

To realize the dimensions of the love of God, its breadth, and length, and depth, and height, will serve to drive home to us the reality of God's love, and the result of our belief in that love will be that no question will ever profoundly vex our minds, no sorrow overwhelm our spirits, because our heart is at rest in God, just as the heart of our Lord was at rest in His Father. This does not mean that our faith will not be tested; if it is faith, it must be tested, but, profoundly speaking, it will be supremely easy to believe in God.

My Utmost for His Highest
by *Oswald Chambers*
   The classic devotional bestseller. These powerful words will refresh those who need encouragement, brighten the way of those in difficulty, and strengthen personal relationships with Christ. A book to use every day for the rest of your life.

Audio Tape Edition: The complete work on twelve cassettes.

The Oswald Chambers Library
   Powerful insights on topics of interest to every believer:

Shade of His Hand
   A challenging look at Ecclesiastes.

Bringing Sons Into Glory/Making All Things New
   The glories of the great truths of salvation and redemption.

Baffled to Fight Better
   Job and the problem of suffering.

If You Will Ask
   Reflections on the power of prayer.

The Love of God
   An intimate look at the Father-heart of God.

Not Knowing Where
   Keen spiritual direction through knowing and trusting God.

The Place of Help
   Thoughts on daily needs of the Christian life.

Order from your favorite bookstore or from:

DISCOVERY HOUSE PUBLISHERS
Box 3566
Grand Rapids, MI 49501
Call toll-free: 1-800-283-8333

Note to the Reader

The publisher invites you to share your response to the message of this book by writing Discovery House Publishers, P.O. Box 3566, Grand Rapids, MI 49501, U.S.A. or by calling 1-800-283-8333. For more information about other Discovery House publications, contact us at the same address and phone number.